Helping Others Overcome Addictions

D1407730

Helping Others Overcome Addictions

STEVE McVEY and MIKE QUARLES

HARVEST HOUSE PUBLISHERS
EUGENE, OREGON

Cover by Koechel Peterson & Associates Inc., Minneapolis, Minnesota

Cover photo © Hemera/Thinkstock

Back-cover author photo of Mike Quarles by Vernon Terrell

===================== Advisory =====================

This book is not intended to take the place of sound professional advice, medical or otherwise. Neither the author nor the publisher assumes any liability for possible adverse consequences as a result of the information contained herein.

HELPING OTHERS OVERCOME ADDICTIONS
Copyright © 2012 by Steve McVey and Mike Quarles
Published by Harvest House Publishers
Eugene, Oregon 97402
www.harvesthousepublishers.com

Library of Congress Cataloging-in-Publication Data

McVey, Steve, 1954-
Helping others overcome addictions / Steve McVey and Mike Quarles.
p. cm.
ISBN 978-0-7369-4746-6 (pbk.)
ISBN 978-0-7369-4747-3 (eBook)
1. Church work with recovering addicts. 2. Recovering addicts--Religious life. I. Quarles, Mike. II. Title.
BV4460.3.M38 2012
259'.429—dc23

2011050763

Printed in the United States of America

12 13 14 15 16 17 18 19 20 / VP-SK / 10 9 8 7 6 5 4 3 2 1

To my wife, Julia, who has always been there with unwavering love in my journey to freedom in Christ.

—Mike Quarles

To my sons, Andrew and David, whose constant faith in all the highs and lows of life has never been anything less than exemplary.

—Steve McVey

Acknowledgments

To Brennan Manning, who introduced me to grace; to the memory of Bill Gillham, who opened the door to freedom; to Tom Grady, who gave someone like me with a checkered past an opportunity to minister; to Neil Anderson, who had enough faith in me to coauthor four books with me.

And to Herb Sims, my pastor and friend, who always confronts and challenges me with the stark truths of grace; to Vernon Terrell, who co-labors with me in the webinars and makes them possible; to all my supporters, who have made it possible for me to be in this ministry; and to Steve McVey, with whom I have the privilege of ministering the truth that sets us free.

—*Mike Quarles*

My ministry has been a team effort since the day I left the pastorate in 1994. Much gratitude goes to the GraceWalk team, who are co-laborers together with me in spreading the wonderful message of our Father's redemptive and restorative love. From our GraceWalk group leaders to our staff members, each one encourages, impacts, and inspires me.

My wife, Melanie, has always been my greatest counselor, encourager, and example of Christlikeness. Add to that the unsurpassed qualities she possesses as a precious wife, and no man could be more blessed.

It was from Mike Quarles's personal story that I first heard the wonders of grace. What an honor to now be coauthoring a book with him!

Finally, I must acknowledge my heavenly Father and His loving grace. It is from Him that any good in my life has come.

—*Steve McVey*

Contents

Part 1:
The Truth We Need to Help People
Find Freedom from Addictive Behavior

Part 2:
Practical Ways We Can Point People to the Truth

Conclusion

Appendix:
Format for Freedom

Resources

The Big Myth

t has been 15 years since I (Mike) coauthored *Freedom from Addiction* with Dr. Neil Anderson. I am more convinced than ever that Neil and I clearly presented the truth that sets people free from addiction in that book and its companion resources. But as I've directed a recovery ministry for the last 16 years, I've observed that it doesn't follow that people find freedom when they are confronted with the truth. There must be an encounter with Christ and a revelation of the Holy Spirit.

There are major obstacles to this that very few have any awareness of. The biggest is the myth that most Christians and the church at large have bought and propagated about the problem of addiction and its answer. We (Mike and Steve) address this myth in the first chapter. From there we proceed with the threefold purpose of this book:

1. To address the question of, first, why so few people find freedom from addiction and, second, what has to take place before this can happen in their lives and they can go to help others find freedom from addictive behavior.

2. To present the truth that God has already provided the answer for addiction, what that answer is, and how it can be experienced.

3. To show the way you can help those struggling with addictive behavior find freedom and, further, how you can

have a recovery ministry through which people can find true and lasting freedom in Christ.

I (Mike) normally get several calls a week from people looking for Christian treatment centers for themselves or loved ones. Not very many Christians, including pastors, are aware that there are many of them. We have accumulated a list of over 50, but not all of them incorporate the teaching a person needs to know to find freedom. Briefly, that teaching is

- an understanding of grace
- knowing who God is
- knowing what Christ accomplished on the cross and provided for us
- the truth that sets people free
- an understanding of our identity in Christ

Basically, it is comprehension of the finished work of Christ. Our goal here is to set forth what we believe is essential to finding freedom in Christ for the individual and how you can help others find freedom in Christ.

Between the two of us, Mike has nearly 40 years of full-time Christian ministry with more than 20 of it in recovery work; Steve has had over 40 years' experience in ministry. We are laying out our heartfelt passion and vision for those caught in the bondage of addiction and how we can help them.

---⊗∞⊗---

As you get into this book you might start to think, *Why don't they tell me what to do?* Therein lies a major part of the problem. Pardon our Southern, but there are forty eleven dozen Christian programs and thousands and thousands of secular programs that will tell you what to do. However, no one ever got saved, freed, or sanctified by *doing* anything. No one ever will. Five hundred years ago Martin Luther declared that nothing you *do* helps you spiritually.* Only the truth will set you free (John 8:32,36), and our response to the truth must be faith only.

If a program is not firmly founded on the truth you can work it until the cows come home or the Lord comes back, but you will not get free. You may change your behavior for a while and fool a few people (including yourself), but nothing really changes. It may be a valiant effort—religious, noble, and even spiritual—but it will all be in vain and totally futile. Only God can change us, and our part is to exercise faith—that is, to believe the truth of what He has done and what He says. We are saved by faith in Him alone and the Christian life is lived by faith in Him alone. We are also freed from addiction and sanctified by faith in Him alone. "Sanctify them by the truth; your word is truth" (John 17:17).

———

In part 2 of this book and in the "Format for Freedom" appendix, we give you some practical ways to help those struggling with addictive behavior and to set up a recovery ministry for those who are interested. But we implore you to read part 1 first. No one will be able to really help a person until he or she has a biblical understanding of the problem and God's answer for it. If we try to help others without this understanding, our efforts will most likely be counterproductive.

It is not that there isn't a widespread acknowledgment of the addiction problem. There are more programs available and more money thrown at the problem than ever before. Is it getting any better? No, it is worse than it has ever been. It is an epidemic here in America and all over the rest of the world. There is a saying in Alcoholics Anonymous that is said to have come from Albert Einstein: Insanity is continuing to do the same thing and expecting different results. Maybe AA, treatment centers, the church, recovery ministries, and rescue missions need to heed this wisdom, because what most are doing is not working.

So we encourage you to do yourself a favor—and do a favor to those you would like to see experience freedom from addictive behavior:

---

* See Martin Luther, *Christian Liberty* (Philadelphia PA: Fortress Press, 1957), p. 8.

Read this book with an open mind. In order to get free a person will have to change what they believe and what they think, because addiction exists only because the person has been deceived and is believing a lie.

Pray that God will give you a spirit of wisdom and revelation in the knowledge of Him (see Ephesians 1:17). That's the only way anyone finds freedom—in Him (Christ). He is the *way* and the *truth* and the *life* (John 14:6). He didn't come to show us a better way. He is *the Way*. He didn't come to give us truth so we could follow principles, steps, or any program to live life and get our act together. He is *the Truth*. He didn't come to give us a better life. He is *the Life*, and He came to give us His Life, which is eternal, abundant, and victorious. Can that really be true? Yes—that is the gospel, and it is true.

Part 1

The Truth We Need to Help People Find Freedom from Addictive Behavior

Chapter 1

The Lie the Church Believes About Addiction

And how it keeps so many from finding freedom in Christ

(Steve) was a pastor of local churches for 21 years. I saw my share of people enslaved in the bondage of addiction. When I first met Mike Quarles and heard him speak, I sat in stunned silence. I wondered if Mike was an anomaly, one of those modern-day miracles you hear about but almost never see in person. After all, here was a man who also had been a pastor; he had been to seminary; he had enjoyed a successful career; he had enjoyed a wonderful marriage—and had then seen it all go away because of an addiction to alcohol. I had heard of stories similar to this—it was nothing new. Men who lose it all because of poor choices they have made aren't that unusual. I had heard of those, but I'd never met anybody who had sunk to the depths Mike had seen, lost it all, and then, despite the stigma and shame of such a fall, had come back to a place of effective ministry.

As Mike described how he had literally become a falling-down drunk and then continued on to tell how understanding who he is in Christ transformed him, I sat transfixed. At that time I didn't know my own identity in Christ. I had my own struggles with the flesh and couldn't shake off the bad habits I saw in my life. Some might think them mild in comparison to Mike's drinking binges, but the truth was that my sins were as reprehensible as his, despite the opinion of the church world to the contrary.

I had earned a postgraduate degree with a focus on biblical counseling, but my pastoral counseling ministry fit the description Mike gave of legalistic counseling. Through the years I'd told countless addicted people the religious things they needed to do to bring them freedom. Now Mike was telling our group that everything I had told these people wasn't the answer. What could I say? The proof was in front of me. I'd seen little success in helping people find lasting freedom from addictions. On the other hand, here was a man who had found that freedom and who was so comfortable in it that he now spoke openly about a past that many would have been ashamed to admit. (That's one of the great things grace produces in a person—transparency.)

In the days ahead, I would come to understand the truths Mike introduced to me in the teaching I heard on that day in the autumn of 1990. My life too would be transformed as I found freedom from my own addiction—the insatiable need to find love, acceptance, and value from others through success as a pastor, which I described in my first book, *Grace Walk*.

Here we are now, almost 20 years later, working as colleagues in the same ministry, pointing many to the Freedom we have both found to be validated by what we've seen of His effect in our own lives. (Freedom has a name—Christ.) Our desire is to see churches become the clarion voice of freedom to all who find themselves enslaved. To be that voice, though, it is important that we get it right when it comes to the message we share. The sad fact is that while the church talks about Jesus Christ being the answer, an outsider could understandably come to a different conclusion by watching the way we usually try to help people with addictions.

I (Mike) read an article in *Christianity Today* that said that nearly every Christian recovery ministry is based on the 12 Steps. Why is that? Why does the church go to the secular to find an answer? Is the problem of addiction too hard for God? It would seem that way. Admittedly, any addictive behavior—from sex, drugs, alcohol, and gambling to workaholism, materialism, and codependency—appears all but impossible to get free from. A Christian counselor once said that most people never change. He is right. In our combined years of ministry—more than 70 years—that has been our observation. Most don't. But some do. That's why we are both still in ministry.

Who are the ones who change? That's what this book is about. It's the ones who don't accept and believe the lie most Christians believe about addiction. Because as long as one believes the lie, their chances of getting free from anything are as good as those a snowball has of not melting in hell.

Is Christ Insufficient?

What is the lie? Glad you asked. The lie the church believes is this: *Addiction is so difficult to get free from that we need more than what God has provided in Christ—and it is up to us to do what we need to do.* *

We know that no self-respecting Christian would ever put it that way, but our actions demonstrate that this is our actual belief. This is the ultimate deception that keeps us from experiencing the freedom Christ purchased for us on the cross, which is our inheritance and our birthright as a child of God. Many believe you need Christ, but you also need something else, such as a program (a 12-Step one, preferably), a treatment center (usually secular), regular attendance at meetings (daily is recommended), and so on.

If we focus on observing principles or
following steps, we focus on self to change
our behavior and shape ourselves up.

Most of the treatment centers and the meetings (secular or Christian) use the 12 Steps. What's wrong with them? Absolutely nothing. We believe that anyone who works the 12 Steps will improve the quality of their life. However, the Steps will not set you free.† Only Christ can

---

* For further discussion, see "The Ultimate Deception" in the Resources at the back of this book.

† For more on this point see "What's Wrong with the 12 Steps?" in the Resources section.

do that, and when He sets you free you are free indeed (John 8:36). No number of steps can lead to freedom unless Jesus Christ is the source from which that freedom is derived.

You can study *Alcoholics Anonymous* (usually called "The Big Book"), the history of AA, and the autobiography of Bill Wilson (one of the two founders of AA) and find nothing in any of them to point you to the person of Christ and His finished work on the cross. What they do point you to is the 12 Steps and what you must do. Here's a truth that would keep us from wandering away: If the message and ministry don't point to Christ and His finished work, consider them good advice at best and error at worst. There is a multitude of very good advice and recommendations out there, but as Paul said in Colossians 2:23, "they lack any value in restraining sensual indulgence."

Likewise, there is nothing wrong with the Celebrate Recovery program's Eight Recovery Principles, which are based on the beatitudes. But there are no principles, steps, rules, laws, methods, or programs that will free you from addiction. The only way to change behavior is by faith in what Christ has already done. What we need to do is know what He accomplished on the cross—and who we are and what we have as a result of that. If we focus on observing principles or following steps, we focus on self to change our behavior and shape ourselves up—"to overcome hurts, habits and hang-ups," as Celebrate Recovery puts it.

The Effects of the Lie

When I (Mike) was struggling with alcoholism, I was a member of the largest church in its denomination. It was probably the most evangelistic and most respected evangelical church in the state. Their initial counsel to me was to go to AA meetings. Later, after I was brought before their discipline committee because of my drunkenness, they sent me to a secular treatment center. I believe that what they did was motivated by love for me and that they truly wanted to help me. If that was so, why do I call their actions "spiritual malpractice"? Why did they not help me? Why would that excellent church send me to a secular treatment center that, because of its cost and my precarious financial condition due to my addiction, almost bankrupted me—and still didn't help the problem? Because they believed the lie that I needed something more than what God had provided.

When I (Steve) counseled people who were addicted, I often gave them the same kind of advice. I was sincere, and my counsel was based on the knowledge I had, but I seldom saw any lasting transformation in the life of anyone who was deeply entrenched in addiction. Most pastors and churches seem to find themselves in the same place I was. They aren't intentionally giving bad advice. They're just telling people what they believe to be true, despite the fact that it does little more than put a Band-Aid on the problem.

We understand that perspective because we believed it for many years. My (Mike's) thinking went like this: *I have been struggling with addiction for eight long, miserable years. I am destroying everything in my life that is good. I've been a Christian for 18 years, I'm a seminary graduate and a former pastor, and I've tried everything I know and everything anybody has suggested. And nothing helps. It seems that the gospel works for my wife. She's a good person and is able to trust God and do the right thing. But I'm too messed up, and my problem is too bad and too deep for it to work for me. I need something different. I need more. I need to go to meetings every night. I need to go to an expensive treatment center.* *

All of the counseling I received told me the same thing. Not exactly in those terms, but I was told that because of my problem I needed something drastic. In recommending I attend AA, one of the pastors of the church said, "You need to do whatever it takes. Gouge out your eye. Cut off your hand." The message came across loud and clear. The answer was for me to do whatever was necessary to become something I wasn't (righteous) and to get something I didn't have (freedom). These are two of the biggest lies Christians believe, and although those who promote them may be sincere, they are incredibly effective in keeping those who are addicted from experiencing the truth that would set them free.

When I checked into my second treatment center I had completely

---

* See "Thirty Things Mike Tried to Get Free from Addictive Behavior" in the Resources section.

bought the lie. I'd given up all hope of being a good Christian. I just wanted to be a normal person. If God had said to me, "I'll let you be a normal person—show up for your job, come home at night, and be a decent husband," I would have accepted it in a heartbeat.

At the intake interview for this Christian treatment center, its director told me, "Maybe one day you could go back into ministry." It sounded like a cruel joke at the time. It was so far-fetched I couldn't even consider it. Not me. The ministry was for people who had it together and didn't mess up like me. I was so ashamed that I begged the director not to tell the other guys in the program I was a former pastor. I believed I had fallen so far and failed so badly that there was no possibility God would ever use or bless me again.

The tragic reality was that as long as I believed that lie, I would wallow in my self-pity and be of no use to anyone. Lies keep people in bondage.

A number of years ago I encountered a prime example of how widespread this lie is among those who are in recovery ministry. I conducted a "Freedom from Addiction" workshop at a meeting of the International Union of Gospel Missions. At one of the luncheons I was seated next to the director of all the rescue missions in a certain overseas country. When he learned the story of my struggle with addiction, he asked me, "What is your personal program to stay free and not drink?" I responded, "In all likelihood, it is essentially the same as yours. That is, to know I'm dead to sin and freed from it, and to trust Christ as my life and live by faith."

The man was incredulous. I didn't have a program of what I did every day to keep me on track and not drink. He believed I was an alcoholic and would always be one. He was certain I was one step away, or one drink away, from plunging back into the throes of addiction. He said it was up to me and what I did to not get drunk. Because he believed so strongly in this, all the rescue missions in his country gave everyone a program of what they should do to stay sober and clean.

The question in my mind was, *Is anyone finding freedom in Christ?* Most likely some were. God is not limited, and He can work in anybody anywhere in any program He chooses. But as Oswald Chambers said, the only valid ministry anyone has is to point people to Christ.

Moving Toward Reality

In Romans 7:24, the apostle Paul directs us to the ultimate answer for freedom. He asks, *"Who will set me free?"* It is significant that he didn't ask "What will set me free?" What you do, follow, or observe will not set you free from addiction. Only a Person can do this. We may find that wise steps can strengthen healthy behavior and indeed be helpful, but anytime we think we need anything else to be a good Christian, a good spouse, a good parent, or a good minister, or to get free or be sanctified, we have bought the lie that we need something more than Christ. We are complete in Him, and you cannot get any more complete than that.

If we look to Him and focus on what He has done, we believe the truth that we don't need to shape ourselves up and get our act together. Why? Because the old self was crucified with Christ. It is dead and buried and is no more (Galatians 2:20). Martyn Lloyd-Jones put it this way:

> Understand that the old man is not there. The only way to stop living as if he were still there is to realize that he is not there. That is the New Testament method of teaching sanctification. The whole trouble with us, says the New Testament, is that we do not realize what we are, that we still go on thinking we are the old man, and go on trying to do things to the old man. That has been done; the old man was crucified with Christ. He is non-existent; he is no longer there. If we but saw this as we should, we would really begin to live as Christians in this life.*

In other words, if we try to shape up the old person who is not there, this is nothing but trying to shape up and improve the flesh, which cannot be shaped up (see John 6:63). There was nothing in the old person that you were that could be shaped up. There is nothing in our flesh that can be improved. So God took care of the problem, and we can say with Paul, "We know that our old self was crucified with him so

---

* D. Martyn Lloyd-Jones, *Romans: Exposition of Chapter 6, The New Man* (Carlisle, PA: Banner of Truth, 1992).

that the body ruled by sin might be done away with, that we should no longer be slaves to sin—because anyone who has died has been set free from sin" (Romans 6:6-7). We were raised up with Christ and are new creations (2 Corinthians 5:17). The new person we are is dead to sin and is holy, righteous, and blameless. We are in Christ, Christ is in us, and Christ is our life. Freedom is our birthright as a child of God (Galatians 5:1). It is not something we have to work for, but something we need to believe is our rightful inheritance. *It is finished!**

The Question of Identity

If a Christian recovery ministry uses the 12 Steps, which most do, then most of them have a person identify themselves as an alcoholic or addict. Is that true? Is a born-again believer, who is a new creation in Christ and one with Him, an alcoholic or addict at the core of their identity? Second Corinthians 5:17 says, "If anyone is in Christ, the new creation has come; the old has gone, the new is here!" No addiction defines a person's true identity. In Christ, we are a new creation and are defined by His Life, not our bad behavior!

The apostle Paul had the best idea when he said, "From now on, let's not know anybody by his or her flesh" (2 Corinthians 5:16, paraphrased). Let's renounce the lie that Christ doesn't completely deliver people from addiction and the lie that Christians are still sin-loving sinners. In chapter 4, we'll take an in-depth look at our identity in Christ. You'll see that what you believe about yourself determines your behavior. And if a person believes they are an addict, they will never be free.

Why are so many Christians unwilling to change their approach? After all, they are committed to Christ and sincerely want to follow Him and help others. The evidence indicates that they are unwilling to change if that change is not in accord with their beliefs. I (Mike) was a prime example. As a full-time Christian worker, a seminary graduate, and a former pastor, I wanted my life to count for Christ. As I struggled with my addiction and my life spiraled out of control, I believed

---

* For a fuller treatment, see "The Finished Work of Christ" in the Resources section.

with all my heart that my problem was that I couldn't do what I knew was right. I believed with all my heart I knew what to do (pray, read the Bible, trust Christ, and so on), but I just couldn't do it. The problem was, I had bought the lie—if I could just do the right things I would get free. I had to change my beliefs (my theology) before I could experience freedom.

> Both of us used to think that having a quiet time would make us strong and enable us to do what is right.

I recently talked to a man who directs a large recovery ministry for both men and women. We were discussing why some people who seemed to be free returned to their addiction. I shared what I believed. The man seemed to agree with me, but at the end of the conversation he said he believed their fall happened because they didn't continue to do what his ministry taught them, such as reading their Bible, praying, having a daily quiet time, and so on. This man, who is a very godly, gifted minister, believes it is up to the person to do the right things to stay free.

We don't believe that. We highly value our time spent with the Lord in the Scriptures and prayer, but it is not what we do that helps us. Rather, it is our faith in Christ. Behaving in a way that is constructive and not destructive is the *product* of freedom, not the pathway toward it.

There were many times I (Mike) would have an hour and sometimes a two-hour quiet time and yet be drunk that evening. Now, we are not advocating giving up a quiet time. But we know that doing it, in and of itself, will not set us free or keep us free. Both of us used to think that having a quiet time would make us strong and enable us to do what is right. We now know that is not true. If I don't believe that apart from Christ I can do nothing and trust Him to be my life, it won't make any difference how long my quiet time is. If what we believe (our theology) is true, we will be free, because truth sets us free and Jesus Christ is the Truth.

Finally—Good News

Most Christians have no idea about how Satan works in the area of unbelief. He is the father of lies and the deceiver, and if he can get you to believe a simple lie, he can keep you from experiencing what is yours in Christ. He can make your life a living hell even though heaven is your destination. Hardly a day passes that we don't hear from a Christian who is going through this kind of hell on earth. No one has ever told them, just as no one ever told Mike, "The problem is not you. There is nothing wrong with you. The problem is in the lies you believe." Nobody has ever told them, "The answer is not what you do, but what Jesus has done and He has done everything for you to be free."

That is *good news*. The gospel is not an announcement that we must do something. It is an announcement of what has been done. The gospel is not an announcement to do or die, or to try your best. It is an announcement that it has all been done. Jesus said,

> The Spirit of the Lord is upon me, because he anointed me to preach the gospel to the poor. He has sent me to proclaim release to the captives, and recovery of sight to the blind, to set free those who are oppressed (Luke 4:18 NASB).

Did Jesus accomplish what He came for? As He was dying on the cross, He said, "*It is finished*"! And you and I are the recipients of what He accomplished. He came to set the captives free and free those who are oppressed, and He has done it. There is nothing we can add to that. All that we can do is share the great, grand, and glorious news that His finished work on the cross has done everything necessary for us to live in peace, freedom, and joy.

Chapter 2

It's Worse Than a Disease

*A biblical perspective on addiction and its
root cause*

Addiction is so pervasive and so difficult to get free from that the world has developed its own perspective on it. They have determined that the root problem of addiction is that it is a disease. This neatly explains the problem and why it is impossible from their perspective to find freedom from it.

In recent years medical studies have offered evidence that suggests there may be a genetic propensity toward addiction in some people. But to summarily relegate addictive behavior to the category of "disease" greatly diminishes hope in Christ for victory over it. A postnasal-drip sufferer will probably have a sore throat, and their behavior will be affected by it, but nobody would assign them an identity based on that condition and suggest they can never be free from it. Or, as a pastor friend of ours said, "I have a genetic predisposition to want to have sex with every attractive woman I meet, but that is just my flesh. It is not who I am."

Many suggest that, because addiction is a disease, you will never be cured or freed from it, and the best you can do is learn to cope. That is why the 12 Steps were developed. Since a person has an "incurable disease" the best they can hope for is to admit it and work a program that includes attending meetings regularly, doing what they should, not drinking or using, and avoiding people, places, and things that might trip them up. In all secular 12-Step programs and many Christian ones the participants are bombarded relentlessly with the notion that if they don't work the program, the only outcome left for them is drink or use—and die.

This is a convincing argument. But is it based on a correct understanding of the problem? If not, no matter how sincere we are or how hard we try, we will not find a satisfactory solution. As the story goes, when the airline pilot greeted passengers over the intercom, he announced, "I have some good news and bad news. The good news is, we are making excellent time. The bad news is, we don't know where we are heading."

But if we start from a biblical perspective on addiction we will see that it is *worse* than an incurable disease. It is spiritual bondage, and programs that rely on what the person has to do just don't cut it. The good news is that God has an answer for spiritual bondage, and "if the Son sets you free, you will be free indeed" (John 8:36). "Free indeed" is not a term you will hear in 12-Step programs, secular or Christian. What is heard in AA, for example, is "Don't drink, read the Big Book, work the program, and go to meetings." When Paul asked in Romans 7:24, "Who will set me free?" (NASB) there was an answer. It was "Thanks be to God through Jesus Christ our Lord!" The answer is *Who* (Jesus), not *what* (a program).

Before we try to have a ministry to those with addictive behaviors, we need to look more deeply at the spiritual bondage of addiction. What is it? What causes it? A biblical understanding will give us a better understanding of what is needed. What is biblical? And what is so basic that if we overlook it, we will be going astray?

What Is Addiction?

The American Heritage Dictionary says, "Addiction is the quality or condition of being addicted, especially to a habit-forming substance." *The Oxford American Dictionary* defines "to be addicted" as "to devote or apply habitually or compulsively." That is a good definition of addictive behavior. Proverbs 23:29-35 gives a colorful description:

> Who has anguish? Who has sorrow?
> Who is always fighting? Who is always complaining?
> Who has unnecessary bruises? Who has bloodshot eyes?
> It is the one who spends long hours in the taverns,
> trying out new drinks.
> Don't gaze at the wine, seeing how red it is,
> how it sparkles in the cup, how smoothly it goes down.
> For in the end it bites like a poisonous serpent;
> it stings like a viper.
> You will see hallucinations,
> and you will say crazy things.
> You will stagger like a sailor tossed at sea,
> clinging to a swaying mast.
> And you will say, "They hit me, but I didn't feel it.
> I didn't even know it when they beat me up.
> When will I wake up
> so I can look for another drink?" (NLT).

Now a rational person might ask, "Why would a person who has just experienced all these bad results want to repeat what brought them on?" There is only one reasonable explanation. Addiction is spiritual bondage. Second Peter 2:19 sums it up: "By what a man is overcome, by this he is enslaved" (NASB). For eight years I (Mike) seemed intent on destroying everything in my life that was good. But at the same time I was trying anything I could—and everything suggested to me—to stop, but I kept repeating the destructive behavior. I remember thinking, *Has there ever been a time since I became a Christian that I've enjoyed getting drunk, that I would want to repeat it? No.* Why did I keep repeating it? I was in spiritual bondage. As I tried and struggled I sank deeper into the addiction.

Addiction does affect your mind, body, and emotions, but the bondage is primarily spiritual. And until that is addressed the best you can hope for is to learn to cope. (See "The Problem of Addiction" chart below.)

The Problem of Addiction				
AREA	NATURE	CURE	ISSUE	RESULT
BODY	Physical addiction	Abstain	Actions	Behavior change
SOUL	Emotional habituation	Cope	Feelings	Improve self
SPIRIT	Spiritual bondage	Cross	Identity	New person
You are a slave to whatever controls you (2 Peter 2:19 NLT).				

Addiction affects the body, and physical addiction is the result. However, this is a very small part of the problem. For example, all secular drug and alcohol programs put a person into detoxification treatment as a first step. In almost every case they are effectively detoxed from the chemical in a week or less. Of course, this does not begin to get to the root of the problem. The solution for the physical part of addiction is to abstain from the behavior of drinking or using. The result of following this solution would be behavior change. As the person is in bondage, however, they are unable to abstain.

Addiction also affects the emotions and results in emotional habituation. The solution for the emotional part of addiction is to cope healthily, and the result of implementing this solution would be to improve oneself, resulting in a behavior change. The emotions and the body are the only two areas the secular can deal with, and those areas are where the majority of the programs in the world have their focus. But unless the spiritual is addressed, there will be no freedom.

How Addiction Develops and Why It Becomes So Entrenched

When we come into this world, we have a few basic needs. We have a need to be loved and accepted and a need to have worth and value. This is the way God made us, and the only way those needs will be fully met is in a relationship with Him through Christ. But we don't have a relationship with Him when we are born, and so we go about meeting these needs the best way that we can. We develop ways to perform, succeed, deal with problems and stress, cope, protect, defend, relate, survive, and so on. We develop a self-life—an independent way of living in our own resources apart from God. The Bible calls it *flesh*.

What Is "Flesh"?

Flesh is the way that you and I have learned to meet our needs for love, acceptance, and worth. It is "learned independence" from God. After we become Christians the flesh still has a powerful pull on us. It is the memory patterns of how we have met our basic needs. It is what has worked for us in the past. When we face stress and pressure we can revert to the old ways of living. Flesh is what makes the world go around. It's what drives Olympic athletes, movie stars, soccer moms, corporate moguls...everyone.

Is there anyone this isn't true of? No, these God-given needs must be met, and the quest to do so drives most people. An article in the *Atlanta Journal* examined the inner life of homeless people. Had they perhaps given up on having those basic needs met? Impossible—that's the way God made them. The article reported that there is an "emerging subculture of homeless people who have created their own identity, language...they don't have any other way of making themselves unique...it tends to set themselves aside, and they feel they have an identity among themselves."*

The way we meet our basic needs for love and worth is where we find our identity. It is where we find our self-esteem. It actually is where we find life—but true life is only found in Jesus, who *is* Life and came to give us life. Sadly, nearly all of the world, as well as many Christians, is looking for life and love in all the wrong places.

As we grow up, face problems, and go through daily life we get messages about who we are from parents, teachers, friends, bosses, and others. At first they only result in feelings about ourselves, but they quickly turn into what we *believe* about ourselves and who we believe we are. As a result we all develop false identities. These false identities come from the world (family environment, hurts, trauma), our flesh (ways we try to live life in our own resources), and the devil, who constantly

---

* The *Atlanta Journal-Constitution,* December 8, 1991.

accuses us and tells us lies about ourselves, God, and what we need in life. They shape all our life and everything we do. As we try to meet our needs by ourselves we develop ways of living based on these false identities. (See the chart "How We Get into Bondage.")

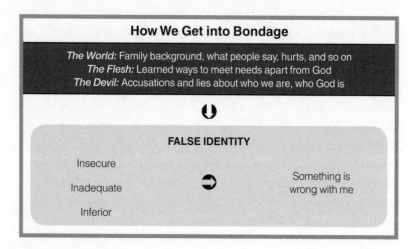

How We Get into Bondage

The World: Family background, what people say, hurts, and so on
The Flesh: Learned ways to meet needs apart from God
The Devil: Accusations and lies about who we are, who God is

FALSE IDENTITY

Insecure

Inadequate

Inferior

Something is wrong with me

We always behave consistently with how we perceive ourselves (who we believe ourselves to be). We wrongly think it is the way we truly are, which is reinforced by one of Satan's biggest lies: *What we do determines who we are.* Some of the ways we behave (flesh patterns), such as irresponsibility, are considered unacceptable by evangelical Christians. Some are considered very bad, such as drug and alcohol addiction. Some are considered acceptable, even praiseworthy, such as perfectionism and being driven to succeed. Our behavior might be good, right, noble, and even spiritual, but if we are trying to meet our needs in our own resources instead of looking to God, we are operating in the flesh. (See chart, "Flesh Patterns from a False Identity" below.)

Strongholds

Some of the ways we behave in order to meet our needs develop into *strongholds.* An addiction or the addictive behavior is simply a mental stronghold—a deep-seated lie that is the result of our misbelief about God, ourselves, and life. Scripture tells us that the stronghold is in our *mind*:

The weapons we fight with are not the weapons of the world. On the contrary, they have divine power to demolish strongholds. We demolish arguments and every pretension that sets itself up against the knowledge of God, and we take captive every *thought* to make it obedient to Christ (2 Corinthians 10:4-5).

Flesh Patterns from a False Identity		
UNACCEPTABLE	VERY BAD	ACCEPTABLE
Irresponsibility	Drugs/alcohol	Perfectionism
Procrastination	Sex addiction	Workaholism
Denial	Eating disorder	Drivenness to succeed
Rebelliousness	Homosexuality	Self-sufficiency
Anxiety and fear	Obsessive-compulsiveness	Materialism
Lying	Codependency	Controlling
You are a slave to whatever controls you (2 Peter 2:19 NLT).		

Consider a true-life story. In 1994 newspapers reported widely on the death of Christy Henrich, a talented gymnast who had narrowly missed qualifying for the 1988 Olympics. She had struggled with the stronghold of anorexia and bulimia since childhood, but in her final five years her weight declined to 100 pounds, then 90, then 70. At a weight of 60 pounds, she died from organ failure, at age 22. How many of her friends and family do you think pleaded with her to stop this deadly and destructive behavior? How could she look at herself in the mirror and believe she was fat? Did she believe a lie? Yes, she believed a lie that resulted in her death.

Here's how believing a lie worked with me (Mike). Many mornings I would wake up and thoughts like these would hit me:

1. I am an alcoholic.

2. I am helpless, hopeless, and I'm never going to change.

3. I am a product of my past.

4. I am different, and my problem is different (so I need a different solution than God's).

5. I am a victim of my family, my environment, my genes, and other influences.

6. I am insecure and I need someone to validate me.

7. I am guilty and condemned because of my behavior.

8. I am a sorry, no-good sinner.

9. I am inadequate and will never measure up.

10. I am inferior to others.

As long as anyone believes lies like these, they will be in bondage. It will not matter how long and hard they work to change the addictive behavior.

A stronghold is a mindset impregnated with hopelessness, which causes us to accept as unchangeable what we know to be against the will of God. This is an accurate description of what every Christian who is struggling with an addictive behavior is experiencing.

The Entrenchment of Addiction

As we seek help for addictive behavior, the counsel we get often focuses only on the wrong behavior and tries to change it. This is the reason we don't get free. The root problem is not the behavior, but the lie we believe about ourselves, which drives the behavior. Eating disorders, gambling, drinking, drugs, and so on are not the problem. They are just symptoms of the lies we believe about who we are, which cause us to try to meet our needs in our own resources (by the flesh).

Why do Christians do this? Why do we still live in the flesh when we have all the resources of Christ available to us? Because we haven't learned or don't know how our needs for acceptance and worth are met in Him. This is the reason that addiction is so firmly entrenched. It is irrevocably linked to a false identity and how we try to find life. That is the reason that no one will ever find freedom until they know and believe who they are in Christ.

Since a person will always act in accordance with how they perceive themselves, most people are trying to change their behavior to get free. They may be trying to change it through spiritual disciplines, but often that is nothing but Christian behavior modification. And that is nothing but legalism, which not only doesn't work but is counterproductive.

Take another look at the chart above, "Flesh Patterns from a False Identity." Now any one person probably doesn't have all of these flesh patterns, but most people struggling with addictive behavior have several of them. I (Mike) have to admit that I had a majority of them. Let's say I concentrate on the alcoholism and am able to quit drinking and get sober. Am I going to be free? Not by a long shot. As long as I cling to my false identity in the flesh, I will live irresponsibly and in denial, rebellion, fear, and so on. But when I learn and believe that I am *not* a failure, an addict—unloved, insecure, inferior, and guilty—but forgiven, accepted, competent, complete, righteous, and secure in Christ, I will begin to change my behavior and experience freedom. (See the chart below, "Who Are You?")

If we truly want to help someone and see any real, lasting change and freedom, we must help them to know the truth of what Christ has done for them and who they are in Him. A person who grasps this will not engage in self-destructive, addictive behavior as a lifestyle. They will change their behavior as they understand their true identity in Christ. (See chart, "True Identity," on page 35.)

We Are Made for God

Addiction is Satan's substitute. It is a counterfeit for intimacy with God. Dr. A.E. Wilder-Smith, an addictionologist, said in a speech,

> Drugs change the nature of consciousness…the reason for the drug epidemic is that we have not taught our children to enjoy God forever on a daily basis. We are made for God— to spend time with Him. People are sensory deprived so they induce spiritual experiences through drugs.*

---

* See also A.E. Wilder-Smith, *Causes and Cure of the Drug Epidemic* (Costa Mesa, CA: The Word for Today, 1985).

Oswald Chambers says that Satan's counterfeit for fullness of the Holy Spirit is drunkenness, ecstasy on drugs, or the sexual experience. That covers the major addictions of alcohol, drugs, and sex. Ephesians 5:18 gives us God's answer: "Do not get drunk on wine, which leads to debauchery. Instead, be filled with the Spirit."

Who Are You?		
Who the world, the flesh, and Satan say we are		WHO GOD SAYS WE ARE
FALSE IDENTITY	⮌	TRUE IDENTITY
Insecure	⮌	Secure in Christ
A failure	⮌	Competent in Christ
Inferior	⮌	Complete in Christ
A guilty sinner	⮌	A righteous saint
Unloved	⮌	Unconditionally loved
An addict	⮌	A child of God
You are a slave to whatever controls you (2 Peter 2:19 NLT).		

C.S. Lewis says, "God cannot give us happiness and peace apart from Himself, because it is not there. There is no such thing." The essence of addiction is self-consciousness. If you have spent any time around those struggling with addictive behavior, you know this is true. They are so self-absorbed they are literally bound up. If this is true, then the answer for addiction is *God*-consciousness. A consciousness of what Christ accomplished on the cross for us and an intimate relationship with Him are the cure for self-absorption. Augustine famously said, "You have made us for Yourself, and our hearts are restless until they find their rest in You."

We believe the 12 Steps and AA have done a much better job of trying to address the problem of addiction than the church has. No matter where you are in the world, you are probably not far from an AA meeting. But you would be hard-pressed to find a meeting that presents

God's answer for addiction in the finished work of Christ. We need to shift the focus from man and the problem to God and His answer. Why did He send His Son? Jesus tells us in Luke 4:18-19:

1. To preach the gospel—good news of what God has done, not what we need to do.

2. To proclaim freedom—our rightful inheritance as children of God.

3. To bring recovery of sight to the blind—so they can see the truth that sets free.

4. To release the oppressed—to take off the burdens of behavior loaded on them.

5. To proclaim the year of God's favor—to proclaim *grace*.

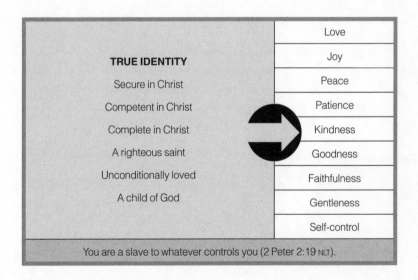

TRUE IDENTITY	Love
Secure in Christ	Joy
Competent in Christ	Peace
Complete in Christ	Patience
A righteous saint	Kindness
Unconditionally loved	Goodness
A child of God	Faithfulness
	Gentleness
	Self-control

You are a slave to whatever controls you (2 Peter 2:19 NLT).

If someone focuses on what they do—their program, their commitment, their group, their steps, their treatment—then their recovery will be limited to their ability to follow through. However, if someone focuses on God and what He has done on the cross, they will be able to experience the freedom that was purchased for them.

When people believe lies about themselves, one of the big problems is that they try to change their behavior, as we have discussed. They wrongly assume there's a "how-to" and believe they can do it. This is a false assumption that leads to a false conclusion.*

What has to take place before a person is convinced that they can't change their behavior and are able to look to God and find His answer? We will take a look at that in the next chapter.

---

* See "There Is Now No 'How' for Those Who Are in Christ Jesus" in the Resources section.

Chapter 3

The Prerequisite to Freedom from Addiction

*What has to take place before a
person can receive their freedom, and
why many never experience it*

Why are most Christians not living free and joyful lives? What keeps Christians from experiencing the freedom that Christ has provided for them? As I (Mike) struggled with my addiction for eight years I asked myself those questions thousands of times.

You might wonder why we're saying that most Christians are not free. Billy Graham has said that only 15 percent of Christians are experiencing the abundant, victorious Christian life. Dr. Neil T. Anderson was recently heard to say that only 5 percent of Christians are experiencing their freedom in Christ. That doesn't mean they are struggling with drugs, alcohol, sex, or some other obvious addiction, but there are many other things that can keep a Christian in bondage, such as co-dependency, perfectionism, fear, depression, workaholism, materialism, unforgiveness, and so on.

Do You Want to Get Well?

Perhaps an incident that is recorded in John 5 can shed some light on why most Christians live this way. Jesus came to Jerusalem, to a pool near the Sheep Gate, where a great number of disabled people lay. Some translations tell us that the people believed that sometimes an angel would come down and stir up the water and whoever got into the water first would be healed. The Scripture says these people were blind, lame, and paralyzed. It seems like a fitting description of many Christians—blind to the truth that would set them free; lame emotionally and out of touch with their feelings; paralyzed spiritually and in bondage.

One man who lay there had been an invalid for 38 years. Jesus asked him, "Do you want to get well?" What a strange and insensitive question! Jesus knew the man had been paralyzed for decades. Why would He ask that question? But if Jesus asked the question we know it was a good one.

We regularly have people call us who are desperate...
When we explain to them what we can offer, we
never hear from nine out of ten of them again.

Albert Camus said in his Nobel Prize acceptance speech, "Liberty is dangerous, hard to get along with as it is exciting." Not everyone wants to be free. Why? We have to let go of all anchors, all our security, all our visible means of support—those things we have depended on all our lives to get by. We have to let go of life as we have known and lived it. We're usually not willing to do this until we are convinced that life does not work our way.

Many people become comfortable with their chains and content with chaos and confusion. Their lives are filled with anxiety and fear. A psychologist once told me (Mike) that I was more comfortable with chaos than peace. I knew he was right, because that was what I was used to, understood, and expected. Often this condition results from family background, and no one was raised in a perfect family. All families have some dysfunction, but some are much more dysfunctional than others.

The greatest fear is fear of the unknown. As a former stockbroker I (Mike) knew that fear of unknown bad news would cause the market to plunge downward much more than when the bad news actually came out. We regularly have people call us who are desperate and want us to meet with them immediately. When we explain to them what we can offer and what they can do to prepare to deal with and resolve their issues, we never hear from nine out of ten of them again. Why? If their situation improves or their spouse or boss cuts them slack, the problem doesn't seem so critical.

It has been our observation that there are three preconditions for a person to find freedom:

1. *Desperation*: a willingness to give up on yourself, your resources, and anything you can do.

2. *A desire to walk with God*, not just get rid of the problem. People often ask me (Mike) if I have a ministry to help people quit drinking and drugging, and my answer is, "No, I have no interest in doing that. I have a ministry to help people get radically related to God."

3. *A dependence on Christ alone*, not Christ plus your program, the 12 Steps, your group, your counselor, or anything else. The subtle deception is, people tend to believe that Christ in them, the hope of glory (Colossians 1:27), is not enough.

In response to Jesus' question, the paralyzed man says, "I have no one to help me into the pool when the water is stirred. While I am trying to get in, someone else goes down ahead of me" (John 5:7). Notice that he doesn't answer Jesus' question. He starts making excuses. First of all, he is depending on the wrong thing—people. He has no one to help him into the pool when the water is stirred. Unfortunately, most who attend programs are depending on the same thing. Second, like most of us he is looking for that special zap to rid him of his problem. The altars of many churches are flooded every Sunday with people seeking the same thing. Lastly, the man as much as says, "I always get a bad break. Someone gets down to the water before me, so obviously God has no interest in helping me."

Jesus overlooks these excuses and heals the man anyway. As the former invalid goes on his way, the Jewish leaders tell him that it is against the law for him to carry his mat. There will always be naysayers, doubters, and legalists who say you can't get free and shouldn't act free. Then they ask him, "Who is the man who said to you, 'Pick up your pallet and walk'?" (John 5:12 NASB). Good question—the answer is the Son, who if He sets you free, you are free indeed.

There Is a Price to Pay

Is there a price to pay for freedom? Yes, there is—it is you, or rather the self-life you have carefully and painstakingly built based on the false identity you have in the flesh. Matthew 10:39 says, "Whoever finds their life will lose it, and whoever loses their life for my sake will find it." Jesus came to give us His life. And we have His life that is now our life, but we are unable to live it until we give up on our life.

What is "our" life? It's the self-life we discussed in the previous chapter—the ways we have developed to meet our basic needs of acceptance and worth apart from God. It is the carefully contrived and persistently practiced ways we deal with stress, face problems, relate to people, find success, avoid failure, and live in dependence on our own resources. Since it's the only way of life we know (other than depending on Christ) we do not find it easy to give up. Many never do. In reality it's not a price to pay, but a burden to release. It's the chains that bind us to a way of trying to find life apart from Christ.

Most people want to get rid of their problems but not really change. It's like the situation of a woman who thinks, *My hair looks terrible. No wonder I feel awful about myself. I've got to get to the beauty parlor and get it fixed.* This woman is on a mission to deal with a major problem and nothing can stand in her way. So she goes and gets her hair fixed. When she comes out of the beauty parlor, she is still the same woman who walked in. Although her problem is fixed, *she* is unchanged.

That's the objective of most people with an addiction. They just want their problem to go away. But God doesn't work that way. He has no interest in removing our problem. His goal for us is that we give up on our self-life and trust Christ's life in us and be transformed. This requires us to ask some questions of ourselves:

"Do I want advice or an answer?" is the first question. We believe most Christians go to church, hear the Word of God preached, and think, *Well, that's good advice. I might take it, I might not—we'll see.* God does have an answer, but we have to be willing to give up on our own methods, plans, schemes, and programs before we can receive it. We must be willing, as Paul said the Thessalonians were: "When you received the word of God which you heard from us, you accepted it not as the word of men, but for what it really is, the word of God, which also performs its work in you who believe" (1 Thessalonians 2:13 NASB).

"Do I want to cope or to change?" is another question to ask ourselves. I (Mike) received a call from a pastor who told me their church had had a Celebrate Recovery program with a hundred people attending and had trained ten leaders. But he had observed that no one was getting free or growing in discipleship. He canceled the Celebrate Recovery program and started using our resources. Overnight, 90 people quit attending, and 9 of the leaders quit. It's not that difficult to show up for meetings, but to give up on your own life and trust Christ is a price most are unwilling to pay. Most people are more comfortable with steps that tell them what to do. Jesus did not come to make us comfortable, but to conform us to His image. It is not a comfortable process as we come to the end of ourselves.

"Do I want to rehash the problem, or do I want resolution?" is a final question. A man called me (Mike) one morning and said, "I stayed up all night reading your book *Freedom from Addiction* and drinking." That is not normally recommended. He said he related to me and my struggle and just wanted to talk about it. He wasn't looking for resolution. We talked for a while and I offered to help him, but I never heard from him again.

The End of the Road, and the Beginning

From time to time I am asked (usually by wives or moms), "When will they ever stop?" My answer is always, "When they come to the end of themselves and their resources." This does not guarantee they will stop, but this is what has to happen for them to come to a place where they can experience freedom.

In this process, most theologians would stress the importance of being conformed to the image of Christ. The problem is, most Christians think it is *their* job to conform themselves and others. Because this is not so, how are we conformed? It seems both reasonable and biblical to say that it is taking place when we are trusting Christ as our life and living by faith in Him and His resources. But that cannot take place until we give up on our life, our self, and our resources.

Hebrews 12:26-27 points to what God is doing in our lives:

> He has promised, "Once more I will shake not only the earth but also the heavens." The words "once more" indicate the removing of what can be shaken—that is, created things—so that what cannot be shaken may remain.

God is going to shake the things in our lives so that what cannot be shaken will remain. And only our relationship with Christ cannot be shaken. God's plan for our lives is to shake everything we are depending on so we will give up on these things and trust Christ. In 2 Corinthians 1:8-9, Paul puts it succinctly:

> We do not want you to be uninformed, brothers and sisters, about the troubles we experienced in the province of Asia. We were under great pressure, far beyond our ability to endure, so that we despaired of life itself. Indeed, in our hearts we felt we had received the sentence of death. But this happened that we might not rely on ourselves but on God, who raises the dead.

This in turn enriches our understanding of Romans 8:28-29, which tells us that God is working in all things for our good, using them to conform us to the image of Christ.

We learn spiritual truth that sets us free, not by acquiring information and amassing knowledge, but by revelation or illumination from the Holy Spirit. The key to revelation is desperation. Only when all our plans and agendas are in the toilet and we are convinced that apart from Christ we can do nothing are we able to receive God's answer. This sounds devastating—and it is—but it is a wonderful place of release where we find our freedom.

The Power of Weakness

What we've just mentioned points to the problem with people who are struggling with addictive behaviors. Are they just too weak? Do they have low morals, bad character, an evil sin nature, or a lack of commitment? Absolutely not! Many people seem to believe that, but they misunderstand the problem and the answer.

I (Mike) once counseled a millionaire who struggled with alcoholism. He was in his fifties, retired, and lived on top of a mountain in a mansion. He had no relationship with his family. His wife lived in another part of the mansion and his grown children would have nothing to do with him. At the end of a counseling session, he said to me, "I guess I'm just too weak to follow Christ." My response was, "John, you aren't too weak—you're too strong to give up on yourself and trust Christ."

I believed I knew what to do to stop drinking,
but just wasn't strong enough to do it.

That's always the issue. You may be too weak to get out of bed, but you're never too weak to trust Christ. It is not an issue of trying to get your act together. It is not an issue of weakness; it is an issue of strength. People believe they can do what they need to do if they can find the right program, counselor, pastor, church, and so on. They will say to us, "Tell me what to do." They say that because they think they can do what they need to do to be free. They are too strong to give up on themselves and trust God completely.

Watchman Nee says, "The secret of deliverance from sin is not to do something but to rest on what God has done."*

It seems that to "do something" is the reflex response of the

---

* Watchman Nee, *Sit, Walk, Stand* (Carol Stream, IL: Tyndale House Publishers, 1977), p. 10, as found at http://files.tyndale.com/thpdata/firstchapters/978-0-8423-5893-4.pdf.

American Christian to a problem. We have also observed that it is the typical response of Christians in the more than 25 countries where we have traveled. Most of the counseling and advice people receive tells them what to do. That's why the large majority of Christian recovery programs, regardless of their sincere efforts and good intentions, are not seeing many experience their freedom in Christ.

For the eight years I (Mike) struggled, I believed I knew what to do to stop drinking, but just wasn't strong enough to do it. When I was in the Christian treatment center, a lot of the guys there had come in off the streets. It was winter, and some would come in and stay until the weather warmed up. Once I was talking to one of those guys and complaining that my roommate had kept me up all night with his snoring. The man gave me a scornful look as he replied, "You would never make it out on the streets."

He was right. I definitely did not want to give that a shot. A few days later, he and his buddy left with only the clothes on their backs to go back to the streets. Does it take a strong person or a weak one to do that? Maybe it was stupid, but that guy believed he was strong enough to live that way without anyone's help. If he had wanted all his needs to be taken care of, all he would have had to do was stay at the treatment center. It was free—not to mention that he was being given help for his problem.

Hannah Whitall Smith wrote,

> Men will undergo painful self-sacrifices sooner than acknowledge that they are utterly helpless…A religion of bondage always exalts self. It is what I do—*my* efforts, *my* wrestlings, *my* faithfulness. But a religion of liberty leaves self nothing to glory in; it is all Christ, and what He does, and what He is.*

In the U.S., a lot of Christians seem to think, *Wait a minute—we're Americans. We're self-starters and go-getters. We can make it happen. When*

---

* Hannah Whitall Smith, *The Christian's Secret of a Happy Life* (Chicago: Moody Publishers, 1883/2009), p. 231.

the going gets tough, the tough get going. That is a far cry from the Christian life. What is a good description of it? Paul laid it out clearly:

> "My grace is sufficient for you, for power is perfected in weakness." Most gladly, therefore, I will rather boast about my weaknesses, so that the power of Christ may dwell in me. Therefore I am well content with weaknesses, with insults, with distresses, with persecutions, with difficulties, for Christ's sake; for when I am weak, then I am strong (2 Corinthians 12:9-10 NASB).

———

I (Mike) and my wife were good friends with a married couple who are now both with the Lord. She struggled with alcoholism and would have psychotic episodes and end up in a mental hospital. Once she was confiding in me about her struggles and said she wished she were more like her husband or my wife, who both usually did what they were supposed to do and kept things under control. I replied, "I don't, because if I move away from the Lord I crash and burn and everyone knows it. I know I really don't have that option."

Life is a system of trade-offs in many ways. If you're reading this book, you had to give up something—probably a little money and some time. And there are other things you could be doing. Likewise, you can't choose to remain the same person and still get rid of your problem, because the same person will act the same way you always have. God's plan is not to strengthen you, but to weaken you. His plan is not to improve you, but to break you of your self-sufficiency. His plan is not to change you, but for you to exchange your life for Christ's life. God is not going to give you anything else, because He has already given everything to you. You have Jesus. You have it all. You are complete in Him.

There is a price to pay for freedom and it is brokenness—the condition that exists when we've given up all confidence in our own ability to manage life. Is it worth it? It's probably the best thing that ever happened to both of us. We would not be enjoying our freedom in Christ today without it, nor would I (Mike) have a ministry or, most likely, a marriage. Mike Harden, a friend of ours who is the director of No Longer Bound, a Christian treatment center in Georgia, put it this way: "I wouldn't take a million dollars for my brokenness, but you couldn't pay me two million to go through it again." That puts it in the proper perspective.

You can't live two lives. You can't live your life and Christ's life. Not until you know that Christ *is* your life and that your life is hidden with Him in God. Not until you know that is the only life you have and you can say with conviction,

> I am crucified with Christ: nevertheless I live; yet not I, but Christ liveth in me: and the life which I now live in the flesh I live by the faith of the Son of God, who loved me, and gave himself for me (Galatians 2:20 KJV).

Chapter 4

The Birthright of a Child of God

God has already provided everything
we need to be free in Christ

H arry Houdini, the famed magician and escape artist of the early 1900s, would issue a challenge wherever he went. He could be locked in any jail cell in the country, he claimed, and set himself free in short order. Always he kept his promise.

However, as the story is told, one time something went wrong. Houdini entered the jail in his street clothes. The heavy metal doors clanged shut behind him. He took a concealed piece of metal from his belt and set to work immediately, but something seemed to be unusual about this lock. For 30 minutes he worked and got nowhere. An hour passed, and still he had not opened the door. By now he was bathed in sweat and panting in exasperation, but he still could not pick the lock. Finally, after working for two hours, Houdini collapsed in frustration and failure against the door he could not unlock. But when he fell against the door, it swung open. It had never been locked at all! But in his mind it had been locked—and that was all it took to keep him from opening it and walking free.*

Almost every day we talk to Christians who are struggling with an addictive behavior, and this is their problem, as we have discussed

---

* Adapted from Don McMinn, *Spiritual Strongholds* (Oklahoma City, OK: NCM Press, 1993), pp. 73-74.

previously. They believe the lie that they are addicts and in bondage. They do not believe they are dead to sin and freed from it. They know that Christ died to set them free (see Galatians 5:1), but Satan has used their failures, sins, and setbacks to convince them that they're addicts. As Ed Silvoso puts it, they have a mindset impregnated with hopelessness that causes them to accept as unchangeable what they know is not God's will. Harry Houdini believed the lie that the door was locked when it was not. It didn't have to be locked for him to be in bondage. All that needed to happen was for him to believe he couldn't unlock it and get free.

Many, if not most, people believe that the door to freedom is locked and there is something they must do to open it. They believe this because they do not feel free and do not experience it consistently. The solution is not to *do* something but instead to *believe* the truth. The Christian who is struggling with addictive behavior is trying to be someone he already is—a righteous child of God who is dead to sin. He is trying to get something he already has—freedom from sin.

I knew in that moment I was dead to
sin and free from addiction.

I (Mike) recall the day I found my freedom from addiction. It was 1988. I had been drunk the night before and woke up with a hangover. My wife was sick of my behavior and me and had implored me to give her some space, so I was driving up to visit some friends out of town. As I was driving along I was listening to a tape by Bible teacher Bill Gillham from a series called "Victorious Christian Living."* The title of the tape was "Co-crucifixion Is Past Tense." The teaching came from Romans 6. The first two verses say, "What shall we say, then? Shall we

---

* We highly recommend Bill Gillham's book *Lifetime Guarantee* (Eugene, OR: Harvest House Publishers, 1993).

go on sinning so that grace may increase? By no means! We are those who have died to sin; how can we live in it any longer?" Gillham said, "You're dead to sin. I know you don't feel dead to sin, you don't act dead to sin, you don't even look dead to sin, but God says you're dead to sin."

I remember thinking, *I'm not really dead to sin—that's just a positional truth. That's just what God says; it's only how God sees me.* Then it hit me: *Truth is what God says, regardless of your feelings. Reality is how God sees you, regardless of your actions.* I knew in that moment I was dead to sin and free from addiction.

How Do We See Ourselves?

We evangelicals have done what we have accused others of doing. We accuse them of basing their theology on their feelings and experiences, but we have done the same. How many of us could say, "I know I'm dead to sin because I feel I'm dead to sin"? Who could say, "I know I'm dead to sin and freed from it because of my experiences"? None of us could do that, because our feelings and experiences tell us we are very much alive to sin, and many of us are mired in addiction and living in misery and despair.

Perhaps you're thinking right now, *Even though Scripture says we're dead to sin, there is a problem with that. I still do sin, and I have an addiction, besetting sin, or life-controlling struggle.* This does happen, but it happens because we regard ourselves by our flesh rather than as who we are in Christ. And the flesh is not who we are. First Corinthians 6:9-11 clears it up:

> Do not be deceived: Neither the sexually immoral nor idolaters nor adulterers nor men who have sex with men nor thieves nor the greedy nor drunkards nor slanderers nor swindlers will inherit the kingdom of God. And that is what some of you *were*. But you were washed, you were sanctified, you were justified in the name of the Lord Jesus Christ and by the Spirit of our God.

That is what some of us *were*, but that is not who we *are* now. Something drastic and radical has taken place. The ultimate, life-changing, and momentous event in history has taken place—the finished work of Christ. If we do not view life and interpret Scripture within this context, we will go astray. You have been washed, justified, and sanctified in Christ by the Spirit of God. As 2 Corinthians 5:16-17 says,

> Therefore from now on we recognize no one according to the flesh; even though we have known Christ according to the flesh, yet now we know Him in this way no longer. Therefore if anyone is in Christ, he is a new creature; the old things passed away; behold, new things have come (NASB).

We should not regard anybody according to the flesh and certainly not ourselves, because if we do we will live defeated lives and be in bondage. We should see other people and ourselves as our God sees us.

A close look at the first seven verses of Romans 6 shows very clearly that God has done everything for us to be free from sin. Look at the verbs in this passage and you will notice they are all in the past tense. It is finished. Our freedom has been provided. It is an accomplished fact. It is a done deal. What is our proper response? "If we died with Christ, we believe that we will also live with him," as Romans 6:8 tells us.

If everything has been done, then the only proper response is to believe. Romans 6:6 says, "Our old man was crucified with Him, that the body of sin might be done away with, that we should no longer be slaves of sin" (NKJV). Martyn Lloyd-Jones asks, "What then does Paul mean by the old man? It seems to me quite plain…The old man is the man I used to be in Adam…It is the man I used to be, but which I am no longer." If you know the old man—the old self you used to be— died, you will experience freedom. Why? Because you are a new person and you are free.

Experiencing What Is True

Romans 6:11 summarizes what we are to believe: "Count yourselves dead to sin but alive to God in Christ Jesus." The King James Version words this as "reckon" yourselves dead to sin. It seems a lot of us look at the word *reckon* like we do in the South when we say, "I reckon it might rain tomorrow." We really don't know—it's something less than an educated guess. However, the Greek word *logizomai,* used here and elsewhere in the New Testament, is an accounting term—a mathematical, precise word. It means it is as good as done. It is money in the bank and you can count on it. A direct deposit has been made, and it is a fact you can believe. But if we don't believe the deposit has been made, we don't count on it. We don't withdraw it or write a check on it. So we don't live in the reality that we are dead to sin and freed from it.

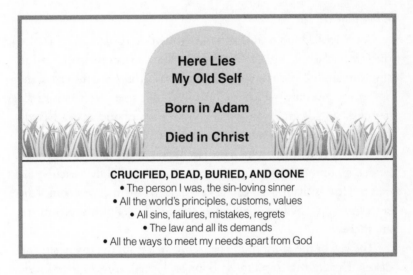

**Here Lies
My Old Self**

Born in Adam

Died in Christ

CRUCIFIED, DEAD, BURIED, AND GONE
- The person I was, the sin-loving sinner
- All the world's principles, customs, values
- All sins, failures, mistakes, regrets
- The law and all its demands
- All the ways to meet my needs apart from God

Count on it: The old self is crucified, dead, and gone, and is no more. Colossians 3:10 says that we "have put on the new self, which is being renewed in knowledge in the image of its Creator." The only experience necessary for this to be true happened 2000 years ago when Jesus died on the cross, was buried, and was resurrected. We were in Him when it happened. We were crucified, dead, buried, and raised up a new creation. "The old has gone, the new is here!" (2 Corinthians 5:17). We're not saying this is easy to believe, but consider this: Do you believe that Jesus was crucified on the cross for you? Why would you believe that? You weren't there and don't know anybody who was there. If you answered, "Because the Word of God tells me so," that is a good answer and the correct one. The very same Bible says that your old self was crucified and buried and you were raised up as a new creation.

You have the same proof for that as you do for Jesus' death, burial, and resurrection.

Oswald Chambers suggests that we have a "white funeral" for our old self and celebrate that he is buried forever. Take a look at the tombstone picture on page 51. Put your name on the gravestone and know your old self is nonexistent—no longer there. The old sin-loving sinner you were is dead and gone.

What Did We Die To?

We have died to sin (Romans 6:2), the world (Galatians 6:14), and the law (Galatians 2:19). Let's take a look at the fact that you died to sin. Romans 8:2 says it is because "through Christ Jesus the law of the Spirit who gives life [which is Christ in you] has set you free from the law of sin and death." Now we all know the law of sin and death is still very much alive and active. All that is necessary is to open our eyes. It is like the law of gravity. Though the law of gravity has not been repealed, we can go to the airport and get on a plane that will fly us across the ocean. How is that possible? The law of aerodynamics overcomes the law of gravity. The law of gravity is still in effect, but is overcome by another law.

The law of the Spirit of life has set us free from the law of sin and death. The door to freedom is no longer locked. It was opened wide when Christ died. Watchman Nee puts it like this:

> Oh, it is a great thing to see that we are in Christ! Think of the bewilderment of trying to get into a room in which you already are! Think of the absurdity of asking to be put in! If we recognize the fact that we are in, we make no effort to enter.*

The Only Answer That Will Work

As we emphasize throughout this book, our identity is the issue. We will always act and behave consistently with who we believe we are.

---

* Watchman Nee, *The Normal Christian Life* (Wheaton, IL: Tyndale House Publishers, 1957), pp. 64-65.

Many Christians attend recovery meetings and believe and confess that they are alcoholics or addicts or recovering ones. If people believe this they will either spend their lives drinking and drugging or trying not to drink and drug. Both are confessions that they believe they are addicts, and these beliefs keep them in bondage.

If we believe the truth of who we are in Christ we can live according to that fact. Now, a lot of people spend their lives trying to die to sin. Both of us did. How do you die to sin? You don't! You have already *died* to sin (Romans 6:2). Our identity is an issue of belief, not experience. Our identity originates in the historical fact of our co-crucifixion and co-resurrection with Christ.

Through Jesus Christ, we didn't get just forgiveness and eternal life. Salvation is not just addition, it is transformation. "God made him who had no sin to be sin for us, so that in him we might become the righteousness of God" (2 Corinthians 5:21). That in a nutshell is the gospel. All of our sins were put on Jesus, and His righteousness was given to us so that we may "be found in him, not having a righteousness of [our] own that comes from the law, but that which is through faith in Christ— the righteousness that comes from God on the basis of faith" (Philippians 3:9). Our new identity is a result of what God has done. We are not products of our past; we are products of the cross. (See the chart below.)

| What You Believe About Who You Are Determines Behavior ||
DECEPTION	TRUTH
I believe my old self is who I am and is very much alive and active.	I know my old self was crucified with Christ and I'm no longer a slave to sin.
I resign myself to a struggle of trying to do what I should.	I appropriate my co-crucifixion and co-resurrection and Christ as my life.
I realize my identity is my flesh and I am a sinner and all I can do is sin.	I realize my true identity as a saint; I am righteous, holy, and blameless.
I believe that because I am a sinner, Satan exercises authority over me.	I understand Satan has no authority; I am dead to sin and alive to God.
I focus on the sin in my life to fight it, but it overcomes me.	I count myself dead to sin and alive to God and live by faith in the truth.
I LIVE IN DEFEAT AND BONDAGE	**I LIVE FREE AND IN VICTORY**

The answers that man comes up with for problems are always based solely on what man does. There is always a program that is designed to change behavior, but it will never be able to do so other than temporarily. The emphasis is always on what man does and his ability to follow through. He must depend on himself and his resolve and resources. (See the chart below, "Man's Answer for Addiction.")

Man's Answer for Addiction
A PROGRAM: To change the behavior
➲ RESULT: self (flesh)-improvement
➲ NEED: To work on doing what we should
➲ DYNAMIC: Our Commitment
SUMMARY: Follow a program of...
➲ LAW: Rules, steps, and principles, through...
➲ WORKS: Disciplined self-effort to...
➲ STRENGTHEN THE FLESH: Improve self to produce...
➲ DEAD WORKS: Behavior change

In God's answer the emphasis is always on what He has done. His answer is not to learn to cope or get by the best way we can. It is always perfect and complete because it is from Him, and He doesn't provide partial answers. It leaves no room for boasting in salvation, sanctification, deliverance, blessing, or anything good that we receive. The freedom He gives comes from placing our faith in the person of Christ and His finished work on the cross. It is not available elsewhere. "Everyone born of God overcomes the world. This is the victory that has overcome the world, even our faith" (1 John 5:4—see chart below, "God's Answer for Addiction.")

As you look over the chart, do you think God's answer would work? In truth, it's the only thing that will work. Although man can do some amazing things, apart from Christ he can accomplish nothing that would qualify as good, loving, eternal, and redemptive.

God's Answer for Addiction
THE CROSS: Changes the person
† RESULT: A new creation with a new identity, who behaves differently
† NEED: To believe the truth of who we are so our behavior will match up with our identity
SUMMARY **OF THE CROSS:** I believe my old self was crucified with Christ and by...
† GRACE: Receive what God did for me on the cross...
† FAITH: Believe I am dead to sin and alive to God...
† SPIRIT: Depend on Christ's life in me to bring...
† LIFE: Good works, the fruit of the Spirit, freedom

The Step of Faith

During World War II, Lieutenant General Jonathan Wainwright was commander of the Allied forces in the Philippines. Following a heroic resistance, he was forced to surrender Corregidor and his surviving troops to the Japanese on May 6, 1942. For three years he suffered as a prisoner of war, ending up in a camp in Manchuria. During his internment, he endured the incessant cruelties of malnutrition, physical and verbal abuse, and psychological mind games. Through it all he maintained his dignity as a human being and soldier.

But after the Japanese surrendered in August 1945, his captors kept Wainwright and the other prisoners incarcerated—the war was over, but the bondage continued. One day an Allied plane landed in a field near the prison, and through the fence that surrounded the compound, an airman informed the general of the Japanese surrender and the Allied victory. Wainwright immediately pulled his emaciated body to attention, turned, and marched toward the command house. He burst through the door, marched up to the camp's commanding officer, and said, "My commander-in-chief has conquered your commander-in-chief. I am now in charge of this camp." In response to Wainwright's declaration, the Japanese officer took off his sword, laid it on the table, and surrendered his command.*

Do you think General Wainwright *felt* free and victorious? He took a great risk when he stepped out in faith, believing the truth. He could have been shot on the spot. But he dared to believe the truth and act on it. It seems that most Christians today are unaware that the victory has been won and has been given to us in Christ. Martin Luther declared, "His victory is a victory over the law, sin, our flesh, the world, the devil, death, hell and all evils and this victory of His He has given to us." In Ephesians 2:5-6, the apostle Paul tells us that we have been made alive in Christ and raised up and seated with Him in the heavenly realm. We are with Him there, at the right hand of God the Father, where He is "far above all rule and authority, power and dominion, and every name that is invoked, not only in the present age but also in the one to come. And God placed all things under his feet and appointed him to be head over everything for the church" (Ephesians 1:20-22).

We—all Christians—are that church. The heavenly realm we have been raised up to, where we have been seated with Christ, is a place of spiritual authority far above all rule, authority, power, and dominion. Where are we? We are in Him. Where are all our problems? They are where everything else is—under His feet. And again, we are in Him. The world, the flesh, and the devil have absolutely no power over us.

Yes, the devil prowls around like a roaring lion looking for someone to devour, but his teeth have been pulled, so to speak. He is a defeated foe (see Colossians 2:15). The world postures and poses and makes a lot of noise, but it is just a death rattle. The flesh continually rears its ugly head, but we can choose to believe the truth about who we are, the truth that sets us free. God has already achieved a full and complete victory. "Having disarmed the powers and authorities, he made a public spectacle of them, triumphing over them by the cross" (Colossians 2:15).

If you are like both of us, you probably wake up sometimes walking

---

* Adapted from Don McMinn, *Spiritual Strongholds* (Oklahoma City, OK: NCM Press, 1993), pp. 73-74.

after the flesh, not feeling dead to sin and victorious at all. One of the major reasons we spend time with God in the morning is to remind ourselves of His incredible grace and love and who we are and what we have in Christ. (We encourage you to read out loud the "Declaration of Deliverance, Freedom, and Victory in Christ" in the Resources section.)

Even though we don't feel victorious, so what? Remember, victory is complete and triumph is total. We know that our lives are often pitiful and our behavior pathetic, but that changes nothing. We have everything, even though Hebrews 11:36-38 tells us that some were put in prison, stoned, sawed in two, put to death, or wandered about "destitute, persecuted and mistreated—the world was not worthy of them." The *Message* paraphrase of 2 Corinthians 4:8-9 puts it like this:

> You know for yourselves that we're not much to look at. We've been surrounded and battered by troubles, but we're not demoralized; we're not sure what to do, but we know that God knows what to do; we've been spiritually terrorized, but God hasn't left our side; we've been thrown down, but we haven't broken.

A Closing Affirmation

A lot of us struggle with financial problems. We limp along in this life, wishing, hoping, even praying for a way out of our financial struggle—like winning the lottery. (As if that would take care of the problem instead of creating more.) However, as believers, we have won the lottery of all lotteries. All sins, failures, mistakes, regrets, and defeats have been forgiven, removed, and taken away. All punishment and guilt, all shame and condemnation and judgment are gone—no more. We have received the Son of God, the Lord Jesus Christ. The Creator of the universe lives in us. He is our life.

We are partakers of divine life. We are in union with Christ. Our lives are hidden with Him in God and we are one with Him. We have everything we need for life and godliness. The Father meets every need according to His glorious riches in Christ Jesus. He has blessed us with every spiritual blessing in the heavenly places in Christ. If He did not spare His own Son, how will He not along with Him graciously give us *all* things? If He is for us, who can be against us? We have received eternal life; divine life.

> The prison doors have been opened wide. Will we
> believe God and by faith walk through them?

If Paul were writing this, he would probably pause and say, "Now to the King eternal, immortal, invisible, the only God, be honor and glory for ever and ever. Amen" (1 Timothy 1:17). The eternal King, the only God, has not only given us an indestructible and eternal life, He has given us Himself. We are indissolubly and irrevocably in union with Him forever, who loved us and gave Himself for us. Nothing can touch us apart from His will. Nothing can come into our lives unless He means it for good. If you are in it, He is in it.

We have received the most priceless inheritance ever given to man. There were no conditions or qualifications. There was nothing for us to do or fulfill. The only condition was to be His child. "See what great love the Father has lavished on us, that we should be called children of God! And that is what we are!" (1 John 3:1). We have inherited His victory, which He won for us at the cross. "Thanks be to God! He gives us the victory through our Lord Jesus Christ" (1 Corinthians 15:57).

We have it all. We need nothing more but to know the truth of who we are and what we have. In his book *The Return of the Prodigal Son*, Henri Nouwen puts it like this:

> As long as I keep looking for my true self in the world of conditional love, I remain "hooked" to the world—trying, failing and trying again. It is a world that fosters addictions because what it offers cannot satisfy the deepest craving of my heart...
>
> Our addictions make us cling to what the world proclaims as the keys to self-fulfillment...These addictions create

expectations that cannot but fail to satisfy our deepest needs. As long as we live within the world's delusions, our addictions condemn us...to face an endless series of dis-illusionments while our sense of self remains unfulfilled. In these days of increasing addictions, we have wandered far away from our Father's home. The addicted life can be aptly designated a life lived in "a distant country"...

I am the prodigal son every time I search for unconditional love where it cannot be found... Why do I keep leaving home, where I am called a child of God, the Beloved of my Father?*

The prison doors have been opened wide. Will we believe God and by faith walk through them and experience what Christ has purchased for us? "It is for freedom that Christ has set us free. Stand firm, then, and do not let yourselves be burdened again by a yoke of slavery" (Galatians 5:1).

---

* Henri Nouwen, *The Return of the Prodigal Son* (New York: Doubleday Image, 1994), pp. 42-43.

Chapter 5

If I'm So Good, Why Do I Act So Bad?

*Why we struggle, fall, and fail—
and why we don't have to*

Probably the question most asked by Christians and the most confusing aspect of the Christian life is this: *If I really am righteous, holy, and blameless in Christ—if that's really who I am—why do I feel like and act like the devil a lot of times?* All of us would have to admit we have asked this of ourselves even after we learned the truth of our identity in Christ and understood grace and the truth that sets free. Why is this?

As we mentioned in chapter 1, a well-known Christian author and counselor said, "Most people never change." This is basically true, and history tells us that it is not disputable. You cannot change your behavior unless you are fundamentally changed at the core of your being. But in Christ, we are new creations. So why don't that many change their behavior? Most Christians, as we've seen, do not believe they are changed and are still trying to change the old self they think they are. They still believe they are the same old sin-loving sinner, alcoholic, addict, codependent, homosexual, anorexic…you name it. They believe their sins are forgiven and they are going to heaven, but they don't believe they are dead to sin, freed from it, and alive to God. So they spend their lives doing their best with their own resources, trying to do right and avoid wrong. After years of futility and quiet desperation many give up the fight.

What Do We Do with Our Feelings?

If what we believe doesn't reflect reality, then our emotions won't reflect the truth and we will be reinforced in believing a lie. For instance, I (Mike) grew up believing you could not trust women; they were all deceitful. My wife was trustworthy, but I couldn't believe it and almost destroyed our marriage with my distrust and jealousy. My emotions didn't reflect the truth, and my actions were based on the lie I believed. Many Christians don't feel free, loved, accepted, and cared for and are in bondage to addictive behavior. They believe what their feelings are telling them. Feelings are real, but they very seldom tell us the truth. We will never in this life feel consistently dead to sin and free from it, but the fact is we are.

Mike received an e-mail from a young man in a Bible college, who is addicted to drugs. In part of his message he said that it had gotten so bad that he was taking four pills a day. He had been through rehab, but it had not helped. The 12 Steps just kept him in bondage, he said, and there was no true deliverance. He had seen on my website that the problem was not behavior but who we perceive ourselves to be. He said he loved Jesus and had given his life to Him, but was wondering why he struggled with something completely contrary to what he was supposed to believe in.

The spiritual bondage of addiction doesn't respond to logic, reason, and clear thinking. It also does not respond to sincere effort and good intentions. Christ has done everything that needs to be done. However, we will not experience this reality by trying harder, but only by faith in who we are in Christ and what He has done for us.

So what about when we fail and fall—when we blow it? We get in the flesh and move into deception. We become like the Gadarene demoniac—not in our right mind, but temporarily insane. We do not have to, but it does happen. It seems to be typical for that to take place, especially for those struggling with addictive behavior.

There is great danger when this happens, because the enemy is there to accuse and condemn us and tell us we are not new creations in Christ and certainly not dead to sin. It is so easy to believe this. And if we do, Satan can take advantage of our failure and plunge us back into the bondage of addiction. What has happened? Actually, nothing has changed except that you have entered into deception. You are no longer living in the truth. You have (in your mind) stepped out of reality into fantasy. The flights that we can take in our minds and the places we can go are amazing.

Taking the Problem Apart

The Bible has a very clear answer in Romans 7. First of all, it seems Paul had the same problem we did, but he also shares the answer with us. His testimony in verses 15-20 is,

> What I am doing, I do not understand; for I am not practicing what I would like to do, but I am doing the very thing I hate. But if I do the very thing I do not want to do, I agree with the Law, confessing that the Law is good. So now, no longer am I the one doing it, but sin which dwells in me. For I know that nothing good dwells in me, that is, in my flesh; for the willing is present in me, but the doing of the good is not. For the good that I want, I do not do, but I practice the very evil that I do not want. But if I am doing the very thing I do not want, I am no longer the one doing it, but sin which dwells in me (NASB).

Can you relate to the beginning sentence? We're sure nearly every believer who has ever lived can, with the exception of Jesus. When we first look at this passage it appears that Paul is defeated and there is no help available. But a closer reading will give us the answer. Paul tells us some very important things:

1. He doesn't want to do the bad behavior, but hates it.
2. He is no longer the one doing the bad behavior, but sin, which dwells in him.
3. Nothing good dwells in him—that is, in his flesh.

In the next few pages, let's take a look at each of these one at a time.

We Agree with God

Paul first tells us that he doesn't want to do the bad behavior and agrees with the law. He knows the law is spiritual and it is good. But when you mess up and really blow it, can you truthfully say that? Of course you can. That's why you feel so bad. You know deep down in your heart that you really do not want to engage in wrong. Every Christian believes this whether they feel like it or look like it. You believe it because it is true. You believe it because God has given you a new heart and has written the law on your mind. If you didn't believe it you wouldn't be so upset and agonize so over your bad behavior.

We have been given a new heart, and God
has written His law on our mind.

This is true of every Christian. God says in Hebrews 10:14-17,

> By one offering He has perfected for all time those who are sanctified. And the Holy Spirit also testifies to us; for after saying, "This is the covenant that I will make with them after those days, says the Lord: I will put my laws upon their heart, and on their mind I will write them," He then says, "and their sins and their lawless deeds I will remember no more" (NASB).

Do I have a wicked heart? Absolutely not! That is an old-covenant reality, but we are under a new covenant. The old self we were is crucified, dead, and buried, and is no more. Jesus Christ lives in us and is our very life. We have been given a new heart, and God has written His law on our mind.

When I (Steve) first heard that my old self had been crucified, I didn't believe it. Then when God revealed the truth to me, I couldn't understand *how* it could be true. I felt like the boxer who went into the ring against a towering opponent. During every round, his opponent would pound him mercilessly. When the bell rang at the end of each round, the boxer would return to his corner and his trainer would say, "Get out there and kill him! He hasn't laid a glove on you." This kept happening each round. "He hasn't laid a glove on you." Finally the boxer told his trainer, "Then you'd better watch the referee, because *somebody* is beating the devil out of me!" We all know that feeling, don't we? But there's an answer.

Who's Doing the Bad Stuff?

The apostle Paul continues in Romans 7:17: "No longer am I the one doing it." The rest of the verse continues, "but sin which dwells in me." Is that a copout? No, it is the truth. You have probably heard the term "indwelling sin" and like most people assumed it was your evil sin nature, which God left in you when He raised you up from the dead.

Not so! Everything about you is totally new, including your nature. You still have the same old body, but that is not who you are; it's simply your earthly container until you go to be with the Lord. Paul goes on to explain in the next verse that nothing good dwells in him—that is, in his flesh (see Romans 7:18). That is a very important distinction. The sin, which dwells in his flesh (his body), is what is doing the bad behavior.

But isn't Paul still the one doing it? No. Who is Paul? Who are you? Are you a physical being who has received a spirit? As long as you believe that, there is little hope you will ever experience freedom in Christ. However, you and I are not physical beings. We are spiritual beings who live in a body.

As author Bill Gillham puts it, the body is just our "earth suit," which allows us to function in our limited time here on this earth. Paul says that he knows the law is spiritual, but he lives in a body of sin, and when he believes he is a physical being and lives in the flesh, then he is in bondage to sin. That's why it is absolutely crucial to understand, know, and believe who you are in Christ.

"You = Your Flesh": Is This True?

Finally Paul says in Romans 7:18, "I know that nothing good dwells in me, that is, in my flesh." Lots of people have stopped at "nothing good dwells in me." That is a tragic mistake and will give you a misunderstanding of the Scripture. Paul says that nothing good dwells "in my flesh." If we could get hold of this truth it could revolutionize our lives. There are many people struggling with addictive behaviors who are fighting as hard as they can to stop, but the harder they try the worse they get. Why? Because they believe their flesh is who they are—and they're trying to shape themselves up and get their act together, which is frustrating and futile.

The flesh, which represents all that we are apart from Christ in us, can never be improved or helped. Galatians chapters 5 and 6 help us understand this. We're told in 5:24, "Those who belong to Christ Jesus have crucified the flesh with its passions and desires." How do we crucify the flesh? By faith. Because we know that the old self was crucified and that the flesh is simply the ways of the old self, we realize we no longer have to live in it. We realize that "the flesh sets its desire against the Spirit, and the Spirit against the flesh; for these are in opposition to one another, so that you may not do the things that you please" (5:17 NASB). We also know that if we walk by the Spirit we will not carry out the desire of the flesh (5:16).

It is absolutely essential that we understand who we are in Christ and that the flesh is *not* who we are, and therefore quit trying to shape it up. Because, as Paul tells us in Galatians 6:8, "the one who sows to his own flesh will from the flesh reap corruption" (NASB), which Galatians 5:19-21 details as "sexual immorality, impurity and debauchery; idolatry and witchcraft; hatred, discord, jealousy, fits of rage, selfish ambition, dissensions, factions and envy; drunkenness, orgies, and the like," but "the one who sows to the Spirit will from the Spirit reap eternal life" (6:8 NASB).

Dealing with Bad Behavior

When you engage in bad behavior it does not stem from your true identity and from the core of who you are. You have moved into deception. And when you do, sin takes over and reigns in your mortal body (Romans 6:12). But that doesn't have to happen if you believe the truth that you are dead to sin and count on it (Romans 6:11). When we move into deception we have bought the lie that we have an empty place in us that needs to be filled with something other than God. That's all sin (bad behavior) is—trying to meet a legitimate need apart from God, a need only He can meet.

As we've noted, there are lots of ways we try to meet this need: drugs, sex, alcohol, money, status, busyness, and so on, and so on. The list is endless. These counterfeits are what lead people into addictive behavior that develops into strongholds. When we seek to do this, Romans 6:16 is clear about what happens:

> Do you not know that when you present yourselves to someone as slaves for obedience, you are slaves of the one whom you obey, either of sin resulting in death, or of obedience resulting in righteousness? (NASB).

Sin always leads to death, destruction, devastation, and despair. All of us have experienced this, and when we do it is so easy to believe Satan's accusations and lies: "You'll never get it together. Just look at you. And you call yourself a Christian." The truth is, we *do* have it together, but we've believed the lie that we don't, and that has resulted in the bad behavior.

"Though outwardly we are wasting away, yet inwardly we are being renewed day by day."

We are not saying that the devil made you do it and you are not responsible. Of course you are. You do have a responsibility, but it is not to suck it up, grit your teeth, and try not to sin. It is to believe the truth that you are dead to sin and Christ is your life—and that you have all the resources you need to live in the peace, freedom, and joy He has provided for you. If we set our mind on the things of the flesh it will result in death, but if we set it on the things of the Spirit it will result in life and peace, according to Romans 8:5-6. The body we live in is dead because of sin, but our spirit is alive (see Romans 8:10). We can't trust our bodies. We can't trust our feelings. We can't always trust our thoughts, because the enemy lies to us and accuses us day and night.

But we can trust Christ in us, who is our very life. How do we do that? Simply by faith, when we believe the truth of who we are in Him.

Our bodies are going to die, but we are never going to die. Jesus said, "Whoever lives by believing in me will never die. Do you believe this?" (John 11:26). We don't know about you, but as we grow older and our bodies wear out we find the promise in 2 Corinthians 4:16 to be comforting. It says, "We do not lose heart. Though outwardly we are wasting away, yet inwardly we are being renewed day by day."

Something Has Been Removed

Our bodies are not our enemies, but as we said, we need to realize that sin dwells in them. Our response is not to wage war against our bodies, but again, to realize that the war has already been won. Colossians 2:11 puts it this way: "In Him also you were circumcised...in a spiritual circumcision performed by Christ stripping off the body of the flesh (the whole corrupt, carnal nature with its passions and lusts)" (AMP).

To *circumcise* means "to remove; to cut off." This circumcision took place through the finished work of Christ:

> When you came to Christ, you were "circumcised," but not by a physical procedure. Christ performed a spiritual circumcision—the cutting away of your sinful nature. For you were buried with Christ when you were baptized. And with him you were raised to a new life because you trusted the mighty power of God, who raised Christ from the dead (Colossians 2:11-12 NLT).

The final six verses of Romans 7 confirm that this circumcision has taken place. We are not miserable Christians with a very active sin nature who will never get it together. As I (Mike) have said, I believed this for many years as I struggled with addiction to alcohol. But when I understood Romans 7:20-25, it changed everything:

> If I am doing the very thing I do not want, I am no longer the one doing it, but sin which dwells in me. I find then the principle that evil is present in me, the one who wants

to do good. For I joyfully concur with the law of God in the inner man, but I see a different law in the members of my body, waging war against the law of my mind and making me a prisoner of the law of sin which is in my members. Wretched man that I am! Who will set me free from the body of this death? Thanks be to God through Jesus Christ our Lord! So then, on the one hand I myself with my mind am serving the law of God, but on the other, with my flesh the law of sin (Romans 7:20-25 NASB).

Thanks be to God that Christ has set us free!

Dealing with the Flesh

So how do we deal with this body in which sin dwells? As we have seen, it has already been dealt with, and the way we deal with the temptations and the lies that bombard us is by faith in the truth, trusting Christ as our life and depending on Him. Romans 8:9-14 spells it out for us:

> You are not in the flesh but in the Spirit, if indeed the Spirit of God dwells in you. But if anyone does not have the Spirit of Christ, he does not belong to Him. If Christ is in you, though the body is dead because of sin, yet the spirit is alive because of righteousness. But if the Spirit of Him who raised Jesus from the dead dwells in you, He who raised Christ Jesus from the dead will also give life to your mortal bodies through His Spirit who dwells in you.

> So then, brethren, we are under obligation, not to the flesh, to live according to the flesh—for if you are living according to the flesh, you must die; but if by the Spirit you are putting to death the deeds of the body, you will live. For all who are being led by the Spirit of God, these are sons of God (NASB).

What an amazing truth! Whatever our feelings may tell us, the truth is that we are in the Spirit. Christ is in us, and though the body is dead, the Spirit of God lives in us. God will give life to our mortal bodies through His Spirit in us. So we are to live by faith, and by the Spirit we put to death the bad deeds of the body. We are the sons of God and the Spirit of God is leading us. All of this is really not something for us to do; we are just to realize that it is so and believe that God is doing what He said He would do. Instead of living in bondage to the flesh and its addictions, we can live according to the Spirit, because we have been given life through Him and He lives in us.

Chapter 6

The Most Liberating Thing You Will Ever Do

Forgiving from the heart: An act of spiritual warfare

H ere's a short quiz to launch this chapter:

1. What is the number-one way Satan robs you of your freedom?
2. How does Satan keep you in bondage?
3. What is the most liberating thing you can do?
4. What is the greatest spiritual warfare you can do?
5. What causes the greatest defeat of Satan in your life?
6. What did the cross accomplish?

If you answered that Satan robs you of your freedom and keeps you in bondage through unforgiveness, move to the head of the class. If you answered forgiveness for the next four questions, we should send your award to you.

———

Although unforgiveness is probably not the first issue that comes to mind when we think of addiction, it is the major area that must be addressed no matter what the problem may be. When a person is taken

71

through the Steps to Freedom in Christ (a process of confession and repentance developed by Dr. Neil Anderson), this step, the third of seven, is always the longest and hardest. But it is also the most liberating one. I (Mike) led many people through the Steps and knew that if they were able to get through this step of forgiveness and would truly forgive from the heart, they would in practically every case find their freedom (even though there were four more steps to complete).

It needs to be said here that a person is able to forgive only by faith. We cannot make a person do anything, including forgive, and it is not up to us to do so. A Christian, who has Christ living in them, certainly has the capacity to forgive, but for some the timing is simply not right. The truth is, we in our own resources cannot forgive. However, since Christ is our life and lives in us, we realize that forgiving is what we as holy, righteous, and loving people do. It is our very nature to do so.

If a person does forgive it seems to break the major hold that Satan has on them, which keeps them in bondage. This is because the lies the person believes about themselves primarily come from the hurt, traumas, and abuses they have suffered at the hands of others.

For example, a friend of ours grew up being told by his mother that she wished he had never been born. As a consequence he believed that he was unloved, worthless, unaccepted, inferior, insecure, and inadequate. When he forgave his mother for what she said and did and also for making him feel this way and believe that was who he was, the power of the lies that were the basis of his false identity was broken. Then he was able to believe the truth of who he was as a child of God: not worthless, but precious in God's sight. He could believe that he was accepted, competent, and secure and that his adequacy was in God.

This is why unforgiveness is such a powerful tool of Satan. And why forgiveness is the most liberating thing you can do. A person is bound by the lies he believes about himself until he is able to forgive all who have wronged him.

One of Satan's Favorite Schemes

You may recall that in 1 Corinthians Paul had to instruct the Corinthian believers to kick a man out of the church because he was sleeping with his stepmother. In 2 Corinthians Paul writes that because the man has repented, the church is to forgive him "so that no advantage would be taken of us by Satan, for we are not ignorant of his schemes" (2 Corinthians 2:11 NASB).

It seems clear that one of Satan's schemes to bring us into bondage is to get us not to forgive. Today, considering the many hundreds of Christians we have counseled, we have found that many are unaware of this scheme. Satan takes advantage of every person who does not forgive, and the result is bondage. Every person we have ever helped who found their freedom had to forgive. All of them had people in their lives who had hurt them in some way. It is impossible to go through life without being hurt.

Likewise, if you are going to experience freedom it will be necessary to forgive those who have hurt you. It is God's way. "Bear with each other and forgive one another if any of you has a grievance against someone. Forgive as the Lord forgave you" (Colossians 3:13). Unforgiveness always leads to bondage.

We say we want justice. Really? One
thing we *don't* want is justice.

In chapter 3, I (Mike) mentioned a couple who were close friends with my wife and me. They had been married for over 50 years and had had a rocky relationship. In their earlier years his priority was money and making lots of it. Hers was social status and material possessions. They divorced. She struggled with alcoholism and would have psychotic episodes and have to be hospitalized. He moved in with a younger woman.

But God worked in the man's life and led him to go back to his wife and remarry her. He had to go to the mental hospital to get her as she had experienced another psychotic break. They remarried, and it was shortly after that Julia and I met them and we became close friends. The woman was beautiful and talented, with a wonderful personality, but from time to time she would continue to lapse and go on alcoholic binges and have mental episodes.

Julia and I loved her and her husband and spent many hours counseling with and ministering to her. Her major problem was that she wouldn't forgive her husband for having lived with the younger woman. During her psychotic breaks she would wander around their affluent Atlanta neighborhood in the rain in just her underwear. Once she told Mike that she would know when an episode was coming on and she was losing touch with reality, but she was unwilling to do anything about it. After the couple moved into a retirement home in their eighties she went out on a drunken binge, totaled their car, and ended up in another mental ward. Unfortunately this beautiful woman went to her grave not having found her freedom because she never forgave her husband.

When someone wrongs us, hurts us, abuses us, molests us, takes advantage of us, or betrays us the last thing we want to do is forgive. We want revenge. Well, that's not Christian, is it? So we say we want justice. Really? One thing we *don't* want is justice. I think we all know where we would be spending eternity if we got justice…and it wouldn't require any warm clothing. But too many of us are like the servant Jesus described in Matthew 18:21-35. The man had a huge debt he couldn't pay, which was forgiven by his master. Then he went out and had a fellow servant thrown into prison because he couldn't repay a small sum that he owed him.

We are forgiven of all our sins and given eternal life. When we then don't forgive it's as if we go out and, after putting a dollar in a vending machine to get a bag of potato chips and getting nothing, we go into a rage and trash the machine because of the injustice done to us.

The Role of Judging in Unforgiveness

One truth that blows us away as Christians is that there is no more condemnation (see Romans 8:1). Because of Christ's finished work on the cross there is no more condemnation, judgment, guilt, or shame. Sadly, a lot of believers live like I (Mike) did for so long—under condemnation, even though there is none. It's as if we think that when we get to heaven, Jesus is going to say, "Mike, come here, we need to talk. Some of your sins were so bad we didn't put them on the cross." Is that going to happen? Are we going to be judged? Not unless the cross didn't work. But it did. Our last judgment took place there, at the cross. This is the truth we now have to lay hold of when we mess up and blow it.

In the novel *The Shack* by William P. Young, the main character, Mack, is given an opportunity to judge and decide which of his children go to heaven and which should go to hell. He says he can't do it, but he is reminded that he has judged many throughout his lifetime. And he has to agree that this is true.

We would have had to agree also. It's impossible to be angry with someone and not forgive them unless you have judged them. Now perhaps your judgment is correct, in that they did wrong, but God is very clear on this: "Do not judge, and you will not be judged. Do not condemn, and you will not be condemned. Forgive, and you will be forgiven" (Luke 6:37). Notice that it says we are not to judge and condemn, but forgive.

Why are we told not to judge? Because God wants us to act like nice Christians? We don't think so. No, it's because judgment has already taken place. Someone else has taken your judgment and also the judgment for all the sins of the world. Many have not received this forgiveness, but it is there for the taking.

If we are able to forgive all those who have wronged us, even if we are not reconciled to them, we can live free of resentment and bitterness. Look at another verse that clearly links unforgiveness and bondage: "In your anger do not sin: Do not let the sun go down while you are still angry, and do not give the devil a foothold" (Ephesians 4:26-27). There is only one way to not let the sun go down on your anger and that is to forgive. As God tells us a few verses later, in Ephesians 4:32, "Be kind and compassionate to one another, forgiving each other, just as in Christ God forgave you."

God has only one remedy for anger and it is forgiveness. If you do not forgive you give Satan a foothold in your life, and if Satan has a foothold in your life, there is bondage in your life that will only be broken through forgiveness. That's why forgiveness is the greatest kind of spiritual warfare you will ever do and the most liberating thing you will ever do.

Forgiveness Among Believers

After we become Christians it seems the people we have the hardest time with are other Christians who don't agree with us or have hurt us. Most likely our greatest evangelical tool is to love, accept and forgive them. "By this everyone will know that you are my disciples, if you love one another," said Jesus in John 13:35. Paul adds that we are to "accept the one whose faith is weak, without quarreling over disputable matters" (Romans 14:1). The greatest thing we can do for another person is to accept them, because it is everyone's greatest need. If you are wondering what you can do to improve your relationship with your spouse or children, there is really not much you can do that they will be able to receive until they know they are accepted by you. Of course, forgiveness goes right along with it. You can't accept people if you are unwilling to keep on forgiving them.

Sadly, there are countless examples of terrible bondage among Christians because of unforgiveness. Two that come to mind are young men I (Mike) counseled. Both were from very affluent families and had graduated from top Eastern colleges. Both had been raised in Christian homes by very domineering fathers they hated and wouldn't forgive. Both were completely estranged from their families. One was living in a halfway house, and the other was living in a downtown rescue mission and later killed himself by jumping off an overpass. They were two of the most severely bound and demonized people I had ever met, yet both seemed to know the Lord. But they were both consumed by anger and unforgiveness, and the enemy harassed them continually and made their lives a living hell.

In our pastoring and counseling we have observed that the bondage of depression is often due to unforgiveness. One of the symptoms of depression is insomnia. Dale Still, a fellow counselor of mine (Mike's) at Grace Ministries International,* struggled with it for many years. During this time Dale was tested, and it was found that his serotonin levels were out of whack, so it was concluded he needed

---

* Grace Ministries International in Marietta, Georgia, is an exchanged-life counseling and counselor-training ministry.

antidepressants. However, when he was able to forgive those who had wronged him, his depression and insomnia went away, and his serotonin levels became normal.

I (Mike) also experienced this myself. When I joined Grace Ministries in 1990 I began suffering from insomnia. After I talked with Dale, I wondered if I was holding on to any unforgiveness, and I asked God to show me if I was. He made me aware that I hadn't forgiven my wife for working so hard to fix me during my struggle with alcoholism. I forgave her that day and went home and slept like a baby that night.

Accepting God's Forgiveness

Have you wondered why some Christians seem very judgmental and critical? Let's return to the parable of the unmerciful servant. When the man was confronted by his master about his debt, he replied, "I will pay it back" (Matthew 18:29). Was he going to pay him back? No, it was a debt he couldn't pay. What was his problem? He resisted and never actually received the forgiveness his master offered him. That is why he could go out and have his fellow servant thrown into prison for the small debt that was owed to him.

What we don't have, we can't give to others. We believe that's the problem with many Christians who seem to be judgmental and critical. They have never completely received God's forgiveness. Is this true of you? Although you might say, "I know I'm forgiven," have you received God's total forgiveness?

Here's a way to check yourself out. Do you accept yourself just the way you are? Nine out of ten Christians say *no*. Now, God accepts you just as you are. You do not accept yourself because you have a different basis for acceptance than God does. His basis for accepting you is the cross. But you may be looking at your performance, your sins, or your failures. In order to accept yourself just the way you are, you must look to the cross and know you are completely accepted and totally forgiven. To do that you must forgive yourself. That may sound a little weird, but if you don't accept yourself just the way you are, it shows you haven't completely received God's forgiveness. To forgive yourself is simply to receive His forgiveness, because you are already forgiven.

> Until you accept God's acceptance and forgiveness,
> your attempt to accept others will just be another
> legalistic exercise that ends in futility.

People who don't accept themselves are unable to accept others, and they treat others the way they treat themselves. They are critical and judgmental. Such people are legalistic and focused on doing right, avoiding wrong, and trying to get others to do the same. They're not the kind with whom you want to spend a lot of time.

I (Mike) understand this, because I was extremely legalistic, judgmental, and critical. But when I was able to forgive myself and accept myself just the way I was (no matter how badly I had messed up), it changed all my relationships overnight. *If God accepts me,* I thought, *good grief—I ought to be able to accept myself and anyone else.* Having done so, I found I was no longer judgmental and critical toward others.

So if you want to change all your relationships overnight, do yourself a huge favor—forgive yourself and accept yourself just the way you are. You will be able to accept others. But until you accept God's acceptance and forgiveness, your attempt to accept others will just be another legalistic exercise that ends in futility. Instead, "accept one another, then, just as Christ accepted you, in order to bring praise to God" (Romans 15:7).

If You Think You've Forgiven...

Most Christians realize they are supposed to forgive, but many are deceived by Satan into thinking they have forgiven when they actually haven't. Below are some typical deceptions about forgiveness.

- Forgiveness is *not* tolerating sin. We never do that in our lives or others.

- Forgiveness is *not* refusing to pursue resentment, revenge, or repayment. That's good, but we still need to forgive.

- Forgiveness is *not* justifying or explaining someone's behavior. Many people tend to do that with their parents.

- Forgiveness is *not* assigning guilt for the offense. Rather, it is taking responsibility for how the offense made you feel.

- Forgiveness is *not* when you stop feeling angry anymore. We're good at denial and stuffing emotions.

- Forgiveness is *not* asking God to forgive those who offended you. He already has.

- Forgiveness is *not* acting like you're not angry. That doesn't impress God and it enslaves you.

- Forgiveness is *not* praying for those who have hurt you. That's fine, but you still need to forgive.

- Forgiveness is *not* saying, "Let's just forget about it." That just dodges the issue.

- Forgiveness is *not* forgetting. You might not think about the offense because you've buried it so deep, but it will consume you eventually.

- Forgiveness is *not* brought about by the passage of time. This never happens.

- Forgiveness does *not* mean a relationship is restored. It takes two to do that, but it only takes one to forgive.

A lot of the above things are good to do, but all of them bypass forgiveness. The Greek word for *forgiveness* means not only "to forgive and pardon," but also "to cancel, leave, and abandon." Forgiveness is an act of faith. It is resolving to live with the consequences of another's sin. It is not using the past against them. When you and I sin and confess it, Jesus says, "What sin? I don't remember it. I have put it away; it's gone." Remember, the justice is in the cross! There is no more condemnation, judgment, guilt, and shame. The last judgment for the Christian was at the cross.

The Act of Forgiving

The following was written by a man who found his freedom in Christ at a conference:

The day the conference was to start I was to be admitted to the hospital for the fifth time for manic depression (bipolar). I had gone to several doctors and tried just about every drug they could think of. I had also had shock treatments. I attempted suicide twice. I spent 30-odd years in prisons and jails. I was a drug addict and an alcoholic. I had been in drug and alcohol treatment 28 times. I had lived under bridges for several years.

I ended up becoming a Christian several years ago but always lived a defeated life. When it came time for my Steps to Freedom session, things were going great until it came to forgiveness. The three things that motivated my life were low self-worth, anger, and bitterness, which were caused by being molested by a priest several times, beaten regularly, and verbally abused.

It took a long time to honestly say I forgave the people who'd hurt me, but when I did the depression lifted and my eyes were opened to the truth in God's Word. I did go to the hospital, and after two days they said I didn't need to be there. My doctors said I was a different person. They had never seen someone change so fast. They said, "Whatever you are doing, don't stop."

One thing to keep in mind is that forgiveness is not primarily between you and the offending person. It's between you and God. Satan wants you to focus on the person and the hurt, but God wants you to look to Him and the cross and see that His Son's death provided forgiveness, release, and freedom. God has provided forgiveness and told us to extend it to others. The ball is in your court.

How do you forgive? Here are a few suggestions:

1. Pray and ask God to reveal to you those you need to forgive. He will do it; He wants you to be free.

2. Make a list of those who have hurt you, what they did, and how it made you feel (worthless, unloved, unaccepted,

insecure, inadequate, inferior, guilty, dirty, no-good, stupid, dumb, and so on).

3. Face the hurt and hate and all the painful emotions. Be sure to list all the ways you felt. You may have forgiven the act, but have you forgiven the person who hurt you for the consequences of their act and how it made you feel?

4. Decide that you will bear the burden of sin and take it to the cross.

5. Now *forgive*. Work through your list name by name. Take your time. Let God bring the painful emotions to the surface. Don't say, "I want to forgive." Forgive the person not only for what they did, but also for how it made you feel. This is what forgiving from the heart means—to forgive for the painful emotions and the lies you have believed about yourself that have kept you in bondage.

You may say, "I can't do it." Who are you? Does Christ live in you? Are you in Christ? Is Christ your life? Can you trust the faith of the Son of God in you to do it? Yes, because that is who you are and what you do. It is your nature to love and forgive. It will be the most liberating thing you will ever do.

Chapter 7

It's Not Up to Us

*We can't free or sanctify ourselves,
but God has already done it*

Even a cursory reading of Scripture makes it clear that when Christ said, "It is finished" (John 19:30), He wasn't referring just to our initial salvation, but also our sanctification—our lifelong growth in Him. The Word of God is clear and definitive on that issue:

- He has given us everything we need for a godly life (2 Peter 1:3).

- He has given us the victory (1 Corinthians 15:57).

- It was for freedom that Christ set us free (Galatians 5:1).

- He has blessed us with every spiritual blessing in the heavenly realms in Christ (Ephesians 1:3).

- We are more than conquerors through Him (Romans 8:37).

- We are always led in triumph (2 Corinthians 2:14).

- We have been raised up and seated with Christ (Ephesians 2:6), who is far above all rule and authority and power and dominion (Ephesians 1:21).

- God has placed all things under Christ's feet and made Him head over everything (Ephesians 1:22).

- Christ is our wisdom, our righteousness, our sanctification, and our redemption (1 Corinthians 1:30 NASB).
- Christ is in us (Colossians 1:27).
- Christ is our life (Colossians 3:4).
- We can do everything through Him (Philippians 4:13).
- The old sin-loving sinner that we were has been crucified (Romans 6:6).
- We died to sin (Romans 6:2).
- We are freed from sin (Romans 6:7).
- We are new creations in Christ (2 Corinthians 5:17).*

Adding to What Is Already Complete

In the first chapter we said that the lie the church has accepted is that *addiction is so difficult to get free from that what God has provided in Christ is not enough—so we need to come up with a program to cope with it.* Herein lies the problem: Anytime we get away from the person and work of Christ we have departed from what God has fully provided and entered into what man thinks is best. It doesn't matter how spiritual or noble it looks. Consider Paul's words to the Galatian believers:

> Since you died with Christ to the elemental spiritual forces of this world, why, as though you still belonged to the world, do you submit to its rules: "Do not handle! Do not taste! Do not touch!"? These rules, which have to do with things that are all destined to perish with use, are based on merely human commands and teachings. Such regulations indeed have an appearance of wisdom, with their self-imposed worship, their false humility and their harsh treatment of the body, but they lack any value in restraining sensual indulgence (Colossians 2:20-23).

If you work the 12-Step program or some other good program,

---

* See also "The Finished Work of Christ" in the Resources section.

it will probably enable you to cope better and perhaps abstain from addictive behavior. But so what? God has something so much better for you. God's plan is for true spiritual growth, the ongoing sanctification that comes as part of the Christian "package." That plan is summed up in Christ in you, the hope of glory. That is the only thing that leads to peace, freedom, and joy.

There is a ton of good advice out there about how to deal with issues and improve ourselves, but that is all it is. There is no divine life in it, and it has no power to change anything. But one who possesses Jesus Christ lives in Him and knows Him, and to know Him is to possess divine life—eternal life—supernatural life in you (see John 17:2-3). It is the only life you have. That life does not have to struggle against addictive behavior.

Most of us know that we are saved by His grace, but after that our focus changes to what we do to live the Christian life.

Does that mean you just sit on your hands and do what some people think of as "waiting on the Lord"? No, but it does mean that you realize and are convinced that "apart from Christ you can do nothing." You can believe that only He can revive and restore you. You can believe that you can press on to know Him and trust Him. You believe that because you are His child He will come to you like the rains that water the earth. You can choose to believe God that you are His beloved, blood-bought, born-again, blessed child—dead to sin and alive to Him.

That is exactly what faith is. Our friend Herb Sims, the pastor of Grace Life Church in Woodstock, Georgia, says the faith journey is not to get somewhere, but to discover who we are and what we have.

We're convinced that many Christians struggle with addictive behaviors and cannot seem to get free because they don't really have an understanding of the completeness of God's grace. Most of us know that we are saved by His grace, but after that our focus changes to what we do to live the Christian life, deal with our issues, and find freedom from the things that keep us from doing what we know we should and being who we know we ought to be. In other words, we believe that salvation is by grace, but sanctification is up to us to obtain.

But the journey of sanctification is not to get something, but to discover who we are and what we already have. Hebrews 10:10,14 captures it when it says,

> By that will [God's will], we have been made holy through the sacrifice of the body of Jesus Christ once for all...For by one sacrifice he has made perfect forever those who are being made holy.

Someone has said that sanctification is just unloading a lot of baggage that weighs us down. But most of us are looking to see what we need to do. Maybe we should call a halt every now and then and ask God what we should *stop* doing!*

Getting an Understanding of Grace

Those of us who have struggled greatly and failed miserably to live the Christian life and then experienced our freedom in Christ often speak of "understanding grace." We have come to believe that an understanding of grace is essential to experiencing freedom. For example, when I (Mike) found my freedom in Christ from addiction 23 years ago, I titled my testimony "The Strange Odyssey of a Legalistic Preacher Who Became a Drunk, Discovered Grace, and Was Set Free."

When we understand that Christ's work was finished once and for all, we understand grace. We understand that freedom is not something to achieve through spiritual discipline, but that we simply need to believe that it is our inheritance as a child of God. It has already been given to us; there is nothing left to do but believe it and say "thank You."

Isaiah 53:4-5 helps us grasp more fully what Jesus meant when He said, "It is finished":

> Surely he took up our infirmities and carried our sorrows,
> yet we considered him stricken by God, smitten by him,

---

* For more, see "The Way to Live the Victorious Christian Life" in the Resources section.

and afflicted. But he was pierced for our transgressions, he was crushed for our iniquities; the punishment that brought us peace was upon him, and by his wounds we are healed.

Christ "took up our *infirmities*," He "carried our *sorrows*," He "was pierced for our *transgressions*" and He "was crushed for our *iniquities*." The original Hebrew for those four words helps us see how complete His work on the cross was:

- "Infirmities" refer to *illness, sickness, affliction*.
- "Sorrows" suggest *pain, grief, sorrow, suffering*.
- "Transgressions" indicate *sin, rebellion, revolt*.
- "Iniquity" is *wickedness and guilt*.

It seems He really has taken care of it all. And He did it for *peace* and so that we might be *healed*. Again, the original Hebrew helps us understand:

- "Peace" is *well-being, wholeness, security, safety, prosperity*.
- "Healed" is *cured, recovered*.

Wow, what a recovery ministry! That sounds a lot better than being dependent on going to meetings for the rest of your life. It sounds an awful lot like He didn't come to help us cope, but to provide full and complete freedom and total healing. As the Amplified Version says, "With the stripes [that wounded] Him we are healed *and* made whole" (Isaiah 53:5).

Grace Doesn't Say "Do It!"

Scripture is clear that an understanding of grace is essential to our freedom. There are two major problems all defeated Christians have. First and foremost, they don't know who they are in Christ; and second, they are overcome with guilt. Both are essentially issues of grace, as our identity and our being guilt-free are a result of what Christ has freely done for us.

This clues us in to what we believe the best definition of grace is: "God has done it." The primary declaration of Christianity—the gospel—is not "do this," but "this happened." Martin Luther says, "We don't do anything; we don't give anything to God, but simply receive and allow someone else to work in us—that is, God."* God is the subject and we are the object. Of course it helps greatly to be a receptive and responsive object.

I (Mike) attended a graduation ceremony at a Christian treatment center. All the men said what they were going to do so they wouldn't go back to their addictive behavior. Part of the program was to memorize quite a few Bible verses. One of the men said what he was going to do to stay clean and sober would be to, first thing in the morning, say aloud all the scriptures he had memorized. He proceeded to recite each one of the verses. I thought to myself that the morning recitations wouldn't do it for him, but if he truly believed the verses and lived by them, that would do it.

Do you see the deception in doing spiritual exercises that are good and depending on what you have done? We highly recommend spending time with the Lord in the Bible and memorizing Scripture, but if our focus is on growing because of our activity and not because of our relationship with God, it will only lead to defeat and despair. It will just be a meaningless exercise. We will be following the Galatian heresy— that is, the mixing of law and grace.

God works miracles because of what we believe,
not what we do. That is what grace is.

After being saved by faith through grace, the Galatian Christians were looking to the law in an effort to sanctify themselves. A group we call the Judaizers had been teaching the Christians there what they needed to do to live the Christian life. The apostle Paul was horrified and said to them, "I am astonished that you are so quickly deserting

---

* Martin Luther, *Galatians* (Wheaton, IL: Crossway Books, 1998), preface.

the one who called you to live in the grace of Christ and are turning to
a different gospel—which is really no gospel at all" (Galatians 1:6-7).
Depending on our own efforts to live the Christian life, get free, and
so on is counterproductive and ends in defeat. That is the result of living by law. However, Paul tells us in Romans 6:14 that "sin shall not
be master over you, for you are not under law but under grace" (NASB).
Certainly there is nothing wrong with the law. The law is holy, righteous, and good (see Romans 7:12). *We* are the problem. We cannot
obey the law, no matter how sincere we are and how hard we try. Only
faith in God, His Word, and His works helps us. The apostle Paul asks
five pertinent questions in Galatians 3:1-5 about our response to the law.

1. *"Who has bewitched you? Before your very eyes Jesus Christ
   was clearly portrayed as crucified."* If we are bewitched it
   is from the enemy, and we are deceived. Lies are Satan's
   primary method to keep Christians from experiencing
   their freedom in Christ. The Galatians were deceived
   into believing that they could sanctify themselves by
   their efforts. Many people believe they can get free from
   addiction by their spiritual activities. That is a great
   deception.

2. Then Paul wants to know, *"Did you receive the Spirit by
   the works of the law, or by believing what you heard?"* We
   all know the answer to that. None of us believe in works
   salvation, but do we believe in works sanctification?

3. He then asks, *"Are you so foolish? After beginning by means
   of the Spirit, are you now trying to finish by means of the
   flesh?"* It's easy to get caught up in doing your best for God,
   but as one preacher said, "Doing your best is just another
   definition of sin." Your flesh counts for nothing (John
   6:63) and is hostile to God (Romans 8:7).

4. Paul then asks, *"Have you experienced so much in vain—if
   it really was in vain?"* When we come to Christ, it changes
   our values, perspective, and our whole way of life. Some of

us lose friendships and some lose possessions. Do we really want to go back to the life of bondage from which we were delivered?

5. His final question is, *"Does God give you his Spirit and work miracles among you by the works of the law, or by your believing what you heard?"* The obvious answer is startling and encouraging—God works miracles because of what we believe, not what we do. That is what grace is. Only God can perform a miracle, so does He need our help? It follows that we are set free not by how we behave, but by what we believe; and that we are sanctified by faith, not by the works of the law. That is some of the best news we will ever hear. It is not up to us to live the Christian life, but to trust Christ in us to do it.

The Usual Question

It is clear that the law cannot free me from addiction. It cannot sanctify me. But if I am not under the law and am freed from it, will it make me lawless? Paul posed this question and then answered it: "What shall we say, then? Shall we go on sinning so that grace may increase? By no means! We are those who have died to sin; how can we live in it any longer?" (Romans 6:1-2). The opposite is true—the only way to live free from sin is to know that you died to it and are freed from it (Romans 6:6-7). Martyn Lloyd-Jones explains it this way:

> There is no better test as to whether a man is really preaching the gospel of salvation than this, that some people might misunderstand it and misinterpret it to mean that it really amounts to this, that because you are saved by grace alone it does not matter at all what you do: you can go on sinning as much as you like because it will redound all the more to the glory of grace. There is no better test as to whether the gospel is being preached than this.*

---

* D. Martyn Lloyd-Jones, *Romans: Exposition of Chapter 6, The New Man* (Carlisle, PA: Banner of Truth, 1992).

The most difficult thing we will ever do is believe God. It's not easy to believe that we are dead to sin, righteous, holy, and blameless, and that God is working all things for our good. But God has given us the mind of Christ so we can believe the truth. "What we have received is not the spirit of the world, but the Spirit who is from God, so that we may understand what God has freely given us" (1 Corinthians 2:12).

A proper understanding of grace requires an understanding of the fact that we are under a New Covenant, as we mentioned in chapter 5:

> By one offering He has perfected for all time those who are sanctified. And the Holy Spirit also testifies to us; for after saying, "This is the covenant that I will make with them after those days, says the Lord: I will put my laws upon their heart, and on their mind I will write them," he then says, "and their sins and their lawless deeds I will remember no more" (Hebrews 10:14-17 NASB).

The New Covenant was instituted when Christ died on the cross, rose from the grave, and gave His life to us. We cannot pick a verse out of the Bible and apply it to our lives without taking into account His finished work. Too many Christians read a verse in the Old Testament or even the New Testament and try to apply it to their lives in an effort to die to sin. But they are trying to do something that has already been done.

What About Obeying the Law?

Similarly, many Christians think it is our responsibility to obey the law. The seminary that I (Mike) attended and the denomination in which I was ordained taught that obeying the law sanctified us. Of course, we had the Holy Spirit in us to help us, but it was our responsibility to obey. But Scripture is clear that Christians were "held in custody under the law" (Galatians 3:23), that we have died to the law and have been redeemed from it, and that we are not under law but under grace.

The purpose of the law is to show us our sin. "It was added because of transgressions until the Seed to whom the promise referred had come" (Galatians 3:19). In Romans 7:7 Paul says, "I would not have known what sin was had it not been for the law. For I would not have known what coveting really was if the law had not said, 'You shall not covet.'" The law shows us that we are in bondage and in desperate need of help. It gets us to despair of ourselves and drives us to Christ. "The law was our guardian until Christ came that we might be justified by faith" (Galatians 3:24).

The law defines holiness but does not give us any power to obey God. Grace, however, "teaches us to say 'No' to ungodliness and worldly passions, and to live self-controlled, upright and godly lives in this present age" (Titus 2:12).

Today many people teach us what we need to do to be sanctified. And mostly they are very good activities—pray, read your Bible, and so on. However, anytime we decide what we must do and begin to attempt it we have put ourselves under law. Romans 7:5 tells us that when we do this, the law arouses sinful passions. The reason it does is that we have taken the responsibility and are depending on what we do, rather than on Christ, who is our life. We are living not by faith, but by works. And our best efforts to do what only Christ can do always end up in miserable failure. We are then plunged into guilt, assaulted by accusations of the enemy, and effectively neutralized in the Christian life.

So if we are not sanctified by our observance of the law and what we do, how will we be sanctified and find our freedom? Colossians 2:6 says that, in the same way we received Christ, we are to continue to live in Him. God provides tremendous resources for us and in us. We access them by believing His very great and precious promises (see 2 Peter 1:4). God works by telling us what He has given us (grace), and we are to believe it (faith).

If we don't understand grace we will be trying everything that comes down the pike from new teachings, groups, events, churches, pastors, counselors, experiences, and so on and so on. But if we know we're complete in Christ (see Colossians 2:10), we know we have all we need. There is no such thing as advanced Christianity. Every Christian begins the Christian life with everything they will ever receive.

However, we will spend the rest of our lives learning what we have, believing it, receiving it by faith, and growing in Christ.

Don't Make God's Grace Useless

There is a fascinating verse in 2 Corinthians where Paul says, "As God's co-workers we urge you not to receive God's grace in vain" (6:1). We receive the grace of God in vain

- when we try to live for God when, in fact, He is living in us
- when we try to overcome addictive behavior and He has already set us free
- when we try to fight against sin and Christ took our sin and became sin for us
- when we try to shape up, do right, and get our act together and we are complete in Him
- when we struggle for victory when it has already been given to us
- when we try to achieve righteousness and we are the righteousness of God in Him
- when we try to get God to bless us and we have been blessed with every spiritual blessing
- when we beg God to give us what we need and we have everything we need for life and godliness
- when we try to get closer to God and He is living in us and is our life
- when we try to abide (remain) in Christ and we are in Him and our life is hidden with Christ in God

Don't receive the grace of God in vain; embrace it, revel in it, rest in it, live in it, proclaim it, and celebrate it. It is the greatest gift you will ever receive and it is all you will ever need. "On that day you will realize that I am in my Father, and you are in me, and I am in you" (John 14:20).

Summing It Up

To be under grace means it is no longer up to you to live the Christian life in your own resources. To be under grace means it is not up to you to do anything to get free from addiction. Earlier we said that a good definition of grace is "God has done it." God has done it; your freedom from addiction has been purchased for you. Whether you believe it, feel like it, look like it or act like it, you are dead to sin. Its power has been broken in your life. "The power of the life-giving Spirit has freed you from the power of sin that leads to death" (Romans 8:2 NLT). Freedom is your birthright as a child of God. It's part of the grace package.

You cannot separate or make a distinction
between God and His gospel and grace.

The only way to get grace is to receive it. You cannot buy it, earn it, deserve it, or attain it. The Greek word for grace is *charis*, which comes from the Greek word *charizomai*, meaning "to give freely or graciously as a favor, with no expectation of return." Romans 5:17 sums it up by saying, "How much more will those who receive God's abundant provision of grace and of the gift of righteousness reign in life through the one man, Jesus Christ!" That is as close to a formula as you will find in the New Testament for living the victorious Christian life, but it's not what most people are looking for, as there is nothing to do. It's all about receiving what God has already made available for us.

Grace is not simply another doctrine. You cannot separate or make a distinction between God and His gospel and grace. Paul understood this when he said, "I consider my life worth nothing to me; my only aim is to finish the race and complete the task the Lord Jesus has given me—the task of testifying to the good news of God's grace" (Acts 20:24). Grace *is* the good news—the gospel. Grace is the way God relates to us, now and always.

Part 2

Practical Ways We Can Point People to the Truth

Chapter 8

What We Can Do to Help Others—and What to Stop Doing

Speaking the truth in love and exercising tough love

S tudies show that every family is affected by addiction in some way, even if just indirectly. Because so few people find freedom from addiction, it remains an enigma and a great frustration to family members affected by it. And in many families it is the cause of great trauma and even tragedy.

As we have discussed, most Christians have bought a lie about addiction—because it is so difficult to get free from, something extra besides what Christ accomplished on the cross for us needs to be done. A primary reason people believe this is that relapse, or recidivism, is so common in all addictive behavior. *Recidivism* may be defined as the act of repeating an undesirable behavior after a person has either experienced negative consequences of that behavior, or has been treated or trained to extinguish that behavior. The Bible describes it thus: "As a dog returns to its vomit, so fools repeat their folly" (Proverbs 26:11).

Why would a person keep on repeating behavior that brings negative and sometimes devastating consequences? We discussed the answer in chapter 2. Addiction is spiritual bondage. Something extra needs to be done about it, but there is absolutely nothing we can do—a miracle has to take place. The good news is that the miracle has already taken place—when Christ died on the cross, was buried, rose, and ascended to heaven. And we were in Him when it happened. Galatians 2:20 makes this clear:

> I have been crucified with Christ and I no longer live, but Christ lives in me. The life I now live in the body, I live by faith in the Son of God, who loved me and gave himself for me.

Of course, before anyone can experience this reality, it must be appropriated personally by them. This, as everything else we receive from God, comes by grace through faith. We're not saying the addicted person isn't a Christian. They very well could be. But a Christian doesn't act or look like a Christian when they are living according to the flesh—in deception. They may believe that Christ died for their sins, but not know or believe they died to the power of sin (Romans 6:2,10-11). As I (Mike) have mentioned, I had been a Christian for 18 years and was a seminary graduate and a former pastor, but I didn't know the truth that I was dead to sin. As a result I struggled with alcoholism for eight years until I learned this truth and believed it.

Perhaps you're thinking, *How could I possibly help anyone with this problem, which is so devastating?* If you know and believe what we have been saying in this book up to this point, you are way ahead of most people, including many ministers and pastors. The answer is much simpler than it seems. It is not easy, but it is simple.

How to Help People

There are hurting people all around you, even in your own family. It doesn't matter who you are or what you know—God will use you if you do these five basic things. It is yet to be seen how much the love of Christ can do.

1. *Accept them just the way they are.* If you don't do this, it doesn't make any difference what else you do. It is truly said that people don't care what you know until they know you care. This is everyone's greatest need. In fact, when people realize how loved they are, they are very close to finding their freedom.

2. *Have a ministry of grace.* Don't try to make people do right. Tell them what God has done for them, how much He loves them, and what He will do for them. We need to know the truth—not what to do. We can't do what's right until we know who we are in Christ.

3. *Tell them who they are in Christ.* Identity is always the issue. If you want to give someone real, positive, biblical hope, encourage them in the faith, and see their behavior changed, tell them who they are. We always act consistently with how we perceive ourselves.

4. *Teach them their authority in Christ and how to resist Satan.* Let them know that Satan is a defeated foe. His only weapon against them is the lie, and they no longer have to let him set the agenda.

5. *Tell them the truth that they are already free and have been given the victory.* Freedom is not something to work for and one day perhaps achieve. It is for freedom that Christ has set us free (Galatians 5:1) and we have been given the victory (1 Corinthians 15:57). A person who understands who they are and what they have in Christ can quit struggling and striving, and live in the freedom and victory Christ has provided for them.

What to Stop Doing

To help a person struggling with addictive behavior, there are some things we can do, but primarily we need to focus on what *not* to do. If you're reading this, you're probably a spouse, parent, child, other relative, or friend of the person struggling. Or like me (Mike), you may have struggled with the problem in the past, and God has now given you a desire to help.

It needs to be said first that if the person is close to you, it is very difficult to speak the truth in love and exercise tough love. However, if you are unwilling to do this you will not be a part of the solution—you will be adding to the problem. Realize that little (probably none) of what you say about their problem and what they need to do has any effect. The person is in spiritual bondage and truly is unable to respond. Further, your threats and promises to take action on which you don't follow through are counterproductive. They reinforce to the person that their behavior doesn't have any consequences. In fact, meaningless threats and empty promises actually enable them to continue what they've been doing. As long as you're doing anything that enables their sinful, addictive, destructive behavior, it really won't matter what else you do.

What does it mean to *enable*? If you stop to think, it should be self-evident. Here are a few things we have seen people do, and this list is not at all exhaustive:

- making excuses for them and their bad behavior
- lying to others to cover up for them
- paying off their bad checks, even forged checks that they have stolen (probably from the enabler)
- paying off their drug dealer
- bailing them out of jail
- paying their debts, fines, and so on
- lending or giving them money
- furnishing a place for them to live
- paying their rent or making their house payment
- driving them places (since they don't have a car or have lost their driver's license)
- buying them gas, cars, clothes, and groceries
- feeding them, washing their clothes, and so on

Don't rely on what a person says they will do. Most people with addictive behavior are very adept at telling you what you want to hear. So you should not help them unless they are taking positive steps to help themselves. And most are good at going through the motions to get you to think they are getting help, but if their actions and attitude do not change, you will know that nothing is different.

Hardly a week goes by that we don't hear from parents who have children living with them whom they are enabling. Many of these children are in their thirties and forties. What's wrong with that picture? If you're in such a situation, perhaps you're thinking, *Wait a minute—do I just kick them out and let them go and live under a bridge?* Only you can answer that. The book of Proverbs speaks a lot to situations like this.* In fact, if you want a good description of a person struggling with addictive behavior, just look up the word *fool* in that book. Here again we are not being judgmental, but when someone is in spiritual bondage and Satan is setting the agenda, this is what their behavior will look like.

Is it possible that God can't get a clear shot at them because you are standing between them and Him?

If you are helping them in any way, such as having them live with you, giving them money, or something else, you should set some rules, guidelines, and boundaries. There should be a zero-tolerance policy, which means that when they don't abide by the rules your help immediately stops and they find another place to live or whatever the case may be. If you make the choice to not do this you are simply saying to them, "Don't pay any attention to what I say, because I will not follow through. Just keep on engaging in your sinful and irresponsible behavior, no matter how it affects me, my marriage, my family, my children, and so on. I will continue to help you destroy yourself and all that is important to you."

One of the flesh patterns of all addicts is irresponsibility. One of the reasons for this is that they have never been made to suffer the consequences of their wrong behavior. Anyone who enables someone in

---

* See Proverbs 3:12; 13:24; 19:18; 29:15.

their addictive behavior is making sure that they don't have to suffer its consequences. Only if people come to the end of themselves and their resources will they find freedom in Christ…so have you considered the possibility that God has been working to bring them to that point and you have been their biggest resource? Is it possible that He can't get a clear shot at them because you are standing between them and Him? Do you really want to enable them to live in a way that is sinful and hostile toward Him?

Exercising Tough Love

Some people think that it is not Christian to exercise tough love, and they should just put up with addictive behavior. But consider what the apostle Paul told the Corinthian church to do with the man who was sleeping with his stepmother and was apparently unrepentant: "Deliver such a one to Satan for the destruction of his flesh, so that his spirit may be saved in the day of the Lord Jesus" (1 Corinthians 5:5 NASB). That was tough love. It was tough, but it was done in love so that the man might be saved. The best thing my (Mike's) wife ever did for me was to kick me out of the house and stop putting up with my irresponsible behavior. As I've talked to many men struggling with addiction whose wives had kicked them out, they have acknowledged it was the right thing to do. Of course, most of them wouldn't admit it to their wives and objected vociferously at the time.

It bears repeating that everyone struggling with an addiction is deceptive and deceitful. They have to be—they have to lie and deceive and live in denial to continue with their lifestyle. They know what you want to hear. They know how to manipulate you emotionally. After all, they have usually been doing it for a long time and have gotten very good at it.

Tough Love with the Right Motivation

If you do decide to stop enabling, know that it will not be easy. If you decide to exercise tough love, there will seem to be many sound reasons not to. Those reasons will seem very plausible, but there is really no good reason to enable sinful, ungodly, and destructive behavior.

However, if you do exercise tough love with the wrong motivation it will backfire on you:

- Don't do it in anger, but because it is the right thing to do. Before you can do that it will be necessary to forgive the person. If you're having trouble doing this, read the chapter on forgiveness again.

- Don't do it to get them to do something. To stop enabling them is probably the best thing you can do to provide a climate for them to change, but it shouldn't be your motivation. Keep in mind that there is a very good possibility they *won't* change—and will have a very negative reaction to you.

Your motivation needs to be because you want to stop enabling someone with addictive behavior to live in a way that is sinful and destructive. It must be because you no longer want to be part of the problem. For them to find their freedom they need to come to the end of themselves and their resources. Only God can bring them to the end of self, but you can choose to stop being a major part of their resources. When you quit enabling you get out of the way, turn the problem over to God, and make it His problem, not yours. You must do it in faith, trusting Him with the consequences. There will be consequences—so you need to count the cost and not despair if things don't work out like you had hoped.

What about providing books, brochures, and so on that you think would help them? You have to be very careful here, as this can be counterproductive. As I (Mike) said in chapter 6, when I found my freedom I realized I still had anger toward my wife because she had tried to fix me during my addiction (although I did need fixing). No one wants to be fixed, and most of us react negatively to the attempt. Peter's instructions to wives who had non-Christian husbands are good advice for those whose spouses struggle with addictive behavior: "If any of them are disobedient to the word, they may be won without a word by the behavior of their wives" (1 Peter 3:1 NASB). However, this doesn't mean you refrain from drastic action to stop your enabling behavior.

Codependency: Half of the Problem

Why would a Christian enable sinful, addictive, and destructive behavior? Is it because they love the sufferer and want to help them? Yes…but primarily it is because the enabler has their own addiction. It's known as *codependency*. Wikipedia gives insight into how popular culture understands it:

> A "codependent" is loosely defined as someone who exhibits too much, and often inappropriate, caring for persons who depend on him or her. A "codependent" is one side of a relationship between mutually needy people. The dependent, or obviously needy party(ies), may have emotional, physical, or financial difficulties, or addictions they seemingly are unable to surmount. The "codependent" party exhibits behavior that controls, makes excuses for, pities, and takes other actions to perpetuate the obviously needy party's condition because of their desire to be needed and fear of doing anything that would change the relationship.

The crucial part of that definition is the last sentence. Codependents act *because of their desire to be needed and fear of doing anything that would change the relationship.* Codependency is a flesh pattern that has developed into a stronghold. It is addictive behavior. A codependent is someone who depends on what someone else says and does for their own acceptance and worth. They have placed their dependence on another person instead of God.

The Christian life is a dependent life, but that dependency is to be on God, the One who gave Himself for us, forgave us, and brought us to Himself. God works in our lives through circumstances to get us to realize that apart from Him we can do nothing. His aim is that we will give up on ourselves and our resources, look to Him, and depend on Him. All circumstances (problems, trials, traumas, and so on) are situations God uses to get us to turn to Him so He can meet our needs according to His glorious riches in Christ.

Usually it is the hardest and most troubling things He uses to accomplish this. With me (Steve) it was what I perceived as my failure as a pastor, which I described in my first book, *Grace Walk*.* For me (Mike), it was my addiction. For my wife, Julia, it was her inability to fix my addiction.

Take a look at the chart on pages 106-107.† Steve and Mike both used this chart when they were counselors at Grace Ministries International. It shows clearly the destructive cycle the codependent engages in and how damaging it is to them. And it makes clear that codependency is an addictive behavior.

Codependency doesn't cause as many visible problems as addiction and is not as destructive, but it certainly messes up relationships and makes the codependent a very miserable person. We are reluctant to say this, but we have seen fewer people get free from the stronghold of codependency than from the stronghold of addiction—although I (Mike) am contacted by a lot more people who are struggling with codependency than with addictive behavior. That's because most codependents are calling not to deal with their issues, but because they want ways to fix a loved one.

We have talked to hundreds of spouses and parents about not enabling, but very few ever follow through and stop. Why? Because codependency is a very powerful stronghold, and they are in bondage to it. So, is marriage counseling perhaps appropriate for an addictive spouse and the codependent one? No, because until they deal with their own issues they are not ready for marital counseling. The problem is not the marriage and their relationship with each other. Instead, they both need to face their individual issues and deal with their own problems.

That applies to any dependent–codependent relationship. Maybe the addict is in denial and doesn't want help, but that shouldn't stop the other from seeking help. Unfortunately, the codependent is usually in denial also and believes that the person with addictive behavior is the

---

* Steve McVey, *Grace Walk* (Eugene, OR: Harvest House Publishers, 1995).

† "The Codependent Flesh Cycle" chart was developed by Scott Brittin, the director of Grace Ministries International in Marietta, Georgia.

THE CODEPENDENT FLESH CYCLE

I. CARETAKER

1. Responds to others by
   - a) Fixing emotions
   - b) Anticipating needs
   - c) Solving problems
   - d) Taking others' responsibility
   - e) Taking care of others
   - f) Trying to be all things to others

2. Feels
   - a) Panicky
   - b) Insecure
   - c) Uncertain
   - d) Needed

3. Needs to
   - a) Rest on self-worth
   - b) Give responsibility back to others
   - c) Take responsibility only for self
   - d) Recognize caretaking flesh
   - e) Look at self-life

Motivation:
Tries to meet needs of needy person in order to be needed, valued, and safe themselves

Transition:
When the needy person fails to respond in the desired fashion, the caretaker becomes the...

Tries to escape

Transition:
Victim becomes caretaker in another relationship

II. PERSECUTOR

1) Responds to others by
a) Threatening them
b) Punishing them, withdrawing sexually
c) Anger/intimidation
d) Silent treatment
e) Violence
f) Using guilt

2) Feels
a) Angry
b) Unloved
c) Threatened
d) Unappreciated
e) Hate

3) Needs to
a) Forgive
b) Give up right to be loved
c) Recognize persecutor flesh
d)
e) Give up the right to have the other change

Motivation:
Tries to force the needy person to change in order to feel secure and valued themselves

Transition:
When the needy person fails to change and meet the persecutor's needs, the persecutor becomes the...

WORTH

III. VICTIM

1. Responds to others by
a) Withdrawing
b) Depression
c) Sleeping/avoiding
d) Giving up
e) Playing helpless
f) Crying
g) Complaining to others

2. Feels
a) Hopeless/trapped
b) Helpless
c) Unappreciated

3. Needs to
a) Recognize victim flesh and believe "I am not a victim, Christ is my life"
b) Make a choice/decision
c) Take responsibility for self, not the other

only one with a problem. But until the codependent deals with their own issue, they will continue to be part of the problem.

How to Pray Without Being Codependent

Should you be praying for the person struggling with addictive behavior? Most definitely. They are in spiritual bondage and need spiritual help only God can give. He may use other instruments, such as people doing counseling, books, and so on, but only He can grant what they desperately need—freedom in Christ.

However, it is very doubtful that your prayers will be effective if you are enabling the person to live in a way that is opposite of God's will for them. And we don't believe you should pray that God would enable them to be successful, but that He would bring them to a point of brokenness so they will turn to Him and find His answer and provision for them. As we have emphasized, 2 Corinthians 1:8-9 gives a key concept. Paul's words make a wonderful prayer to pray for someone in this situation:

> We were under great pressure, far beyond our ability to endure, so that we despaired of life itself. Indeed, we felt we had received the sentence of death. But this happened that we might not rely on ourselves but on God, who raises the dead.

Are we saying you should pray that God would put them under great pressure so that they will despair of life? Yes—so they will give up on themselves and rely on Him, who raises the dead. Isn't that where we all need to be? Until they reach that point it is very doubtful they will experience any freedom in their life.

We also recommend praying 2 Timothy 2:25-26, "that God will grant them repentance leading them to a knowledge of the truth, and that they will come to their senses and escape from the trap of the devil, who has taken them captive to do his will." Because God desires that all of His children experience the freedom His Son died to provide, we can pray those prayers boldly and with confidence.

If the struggling person doesn't know Christ as their Savior, we recommend praying that God will convict them of their guilt in regard to sin, righteousness, and judgment because they do not believe in His Son (see John 16:8-9), along with praying 2 Timothy 2:25-26.

Those Who Refuse to Change

So what do you do if you have quit enabling a person with addictive behavior and nothing changes? If they are a Christian, God has some direction for us in Matthew 18:15-17:

> If your brother or sister sins, go and point out their fault, just between the two of you. If they listen to you, you have won them over. But if they will not listen, take one or two others along, so that "every matter may be established by the testimony of two or three witnesses." If they still refuse to listen, tell it to the church; and if they refuse to listen even to the church, treat them as you would a pagan or a tax collector.

Confrontation

Here is the way the Matthew 18 process can work. When I (Mike) was in the midst of my struggle with alcoholism, my brother-in-law Dan, who was also a close friend, put the above instructions to work. First he came to me and spoke the truth in love, confronting me with my sin and misbehavior. When I didn't respond, Dan brought another brother along and they both confronted me. When I made no response to this they approached the church we were members of. In this case they talked to our discipline committee. The committee called me before them and confronted me; they told me they recommended I go to a secular treatment center. If I hadn't done this, they would have put me out of the church. Although I believe it was spiritual malpractice to send me to a secular treatment center, the process itself was biblical, and God used it to eventually bring me to a point where I could experience my freedom in Christ. I'm very grateful to Dan for doing this, and we remain close friends to this day.

Unfortunately, many churches will not take any action if you follow

Matthew 18:15-17. Don't let this discourage you. God is not limited by the unwillingness of His church to honor His Word and follow His instructions. What you are doing is biblical and what God wants you to do. As you act in faith by not enabling, following His direction, and praying biblically, you are turning the person and the problem over to Him. He is faithful, He loves and wants the best for you and the other person, and He can be trusted. It is up to you to give the problem to Him and trust Him with it.

Intervention

Maybe you have done all this faithfully and haven't seen any response. You could then proceed to do an *intervention*. An intervention is when you and significant others in the person's life meet with them and share what you see in their life, how it is affecting them and others, why you believe it is destructive; what you think they should do, and what will happen if they don't.

It is best if you can have someone to lead it who understands addiction and the truth that sets free and knows how to conduct such a proceeding. Ideally all those involved should meet with the one leading it and be instructed in what to do and what not to do. Unfortunately we are not aware of any who do this from a Christian viewpoint. There are quite a few who do it from a secular standpoint, of course. They usually charge a fee and represent a secular treatment center they will try to get the person to attend. However, I (Mike) have led interventions and am available to do this. You can contact me at the address on page 199 if you would like more information.

An intervention can be done without any training or a leader if you carefully follow some simple directions.

1. Everyone involved in the intervention must be a significant person in the life of the person struggling with addictive behavior. If they are married, a spouse is essential in almost every case. The exception would be if the spouse is also struggling with an addictive behavior and would be unable to speak to them credibly, or if the spouse refuses to take part. Others could be close relatives such as parents or children, or anyone who knows them and is familiar with the problem. Friends, bosses, neighbors, co-workers, and pastors are all possibilities.

Many people are reluctant to let children participate, but they can be the most influential and persuasive within the group. They might be too young, but in all cases children are severely affected and understand far more of what is going on than you would think. I (Mike) led an intervention with a woman in which her husband, pastor, best friend, two neighbors, and teenage daughter were involved. All of them shared with her, but she was unmoved and very resistant until her daughter spoke. That did it. The woman broke down and agreed to do what we suggested. Her daughter went upstairs with her and helped her pack, and she checked into a treatment center that afternoon.

2. Speak the truth in love. Stress the fact that you love and care for the person and that you only want the best for them. Don't tell them what a sorry human being they are. Do not accuse them and belittle their character. Don't say you are sick and tired of them and aren't going to put up with it anymore. The point is to help them, not to give you some relief.

"Love never fails," so "do everything in love."

The main thing you want to do is to share facts and events that demonstrate the severity of the problem. Remember that the problem is not them, but the lies they believe. Do point out their good qualities and how much they are loved, valued, and needed. Do tell them who they are in Christ. Do encourage them that it is not too late and that God wants to set them free and bless them, as they are a dearly loved child of His. Do let them know that when they deal with their problem they will be welcomed back with open arms. No matter how much disappointment and destruction they have dished out, you must do an intervention in love if you want to see results. "Love never fails," so "do everything in love" (1 Corinthians 13:8; 16:14).

3. Before you meet, everyone that is to be involved should write out the points they are going to make. Don't wing it. You are too emotionally tied to the person to do that—and it will derail the whole process. Give facts about specific events that have happened as a result of their addiction: You had a hangover and didn't go to work; I had to lie to your boss; you forgot to pick the children up; you were driving drunk; you didn't come home until…; our finances have been decimated; you cussed out the neighbor; and so on, whatever is factual. Tell them how it made you feel and how it affected you, the situation, and others you know about.

It is okay to be emotional, but stick to the facts. This makes your point far better than a character attack. Each participant should take their turn and share their prepared points. You don't have to read your notes word for word, but you want to be sure to make the necessary points about why they need help and avoid tearing them down.

4. Expect resistance. Do not argue with them. Stay with the facts and your prepared points. When everyone is finished sharing, someone—probably the leader or someone in authority such as a pastor or boss—can share with them what they want them to do. Usually, that is to go to a treatment center and to do so *that day*. The immediate action is important because if they don't do it right then they will come up with a reason not to. Of course, preparations will have to be made with the treatment center you want them to attend.

What if they are unwilling to go to a Christian treatment center but will go to a secular one? We never recommend secular treatment centers, but if that's the only thing they will do, then that can be part of the process. We would advise you to let them do it. Keep in mind, though, that most secular treatment centers are very expensive, and if you don't have insurance the cost can be prohibitive.

5. There must be an ultimatum. Intervention will not work without one. You can do everything listed above, and most likely it will be totally useless without an ultimatum. I (Mike) will not be involved in an intervention without one. Or if you do give an ultimatum but don't follow through, the process will be just another round of venting your dissatisfaction and making empty threats to which they will pay no attention. It would be better not to have an intervention than to have one without an ultimatum. All it will do is reinforce their belief that they can continue with their sinful and destructive behavior and you will do nothing about it.

What should the ultimatum be? That is up to you, but it must have teeth in it. It must be tough love. If the person is married, usually it is that their spouse will leave or the one struggling will be kicked out of the house. If their boss is involved, the loss of a job can be very persuasive. It should probably be something on that order—along with the promise that none of you involved will continue with your enabling behavior and the person should consider themselves cut off from anything that will enable them to continue in their behavior.

But this in itself is not enough. For an intervention to be successful, the ultimatum must go into effect immediately, and it must be one that will cost them something. Usually it is separation from their loved ones and their home. Remember, this is not to punish them. It is to help them. And if you are ever going to help them, you have to exercise the tough love of an ultimatum.

6. Count the cost. As we mentioned earlier, the person with addictive behavior may not respond as you desire. In fact, their response may be the exact opposite of what you desire. Are you willing to accept their anger and animosity toward you, knowing that what you did was in love and to help them? Or do you just want to continue living as you have been and accept the person's sinful and destructive behavior? The sad fact is, most are willing to continue their codependence rather than intervene and issue an ultimatum. Again, if you are setting up the intervention just to get them to do something, don't do it. Unless you can do it in faith, trusting God with the consequences and because it's the right thing to do, don't do it!

However, if you do this and the person has a very negative response, all is not lost. You have acted in faith, trusting God. He can use the intervention however He wants to, and it can be part of His process of change in the person's life. We don't know what it takes to bring someone to the end of self and self's resources, but God does. When you choose to follow through and stop your enabling behavior, you have put them in His hands, and He alone can set them free from their addictive behavior.

7. Remember that it is not up to you to straighten out and fix the one with addictive behavior. Only God can bring them to the point that they will turn to Him and receive the freedom that has always been there for them. Again, only He knows what it's going to take to do that. He loves them a lot more than you do, and you can trust Him regardless of what the person does and how bad it looks. It may very well be that it will have to get a lot worse. Those of us who have finally gotten to that point where we turn to God wouldn't trade it for anything. Your only response is to trust God and act in faith.

Yes, it takes a miracle for a person to stop their addictive or codependent behavior and experience freedom in Christ, but in Christ, you are already a living, walking, breathing miracle. If your friend or loved one who is spiritually bound is in Christ they are a miracle also, and there is great hope for them. If not, you can pray that they would encounter Jesus, the One who gave His life for them and forgave all their sins. Don't pray for them to change their behavior. Pray they will come to know the miracle-working God, who will set them free from sin, the world, the law, the flesh, and the devil. Look to Him "who is able to do immeasurably more than all we ask or imagine, according to his power that is at work within us" (Ephesians 3:20).

Chapter 9

A Ministry of
Grace in the Church

*Welcoming, accepting, loving, caring for,
and attracting those who struggle with
addictive behaviors*

I n the "Format for Freedom" appendix we set out suggestions for procedures and materials to use in a recovery ministry,* but here we want to present general biblical principles that apply to any effort to help people who are struggling with sin.

Meeting the Greatest Need

Above all, it is absolutely essential that people feel welcomed, loved, accepted, and cared for. To be loved and accepted is the greatest of our God-given needs. For anyone who wants to have an impact on others' lives, this is a nonnegotiable. If people do not feel accepted, you will never have an opportunity to share the truth that sets free. People who are struggling with addictive behavior have experienced great rejection and expect to be rejected. If they are not welcomed and feel ignored when they show up, they will perceive it as rejection and you probably will not see them again. They are saddled with low self-esteem and guilt and are living under condemnation. It will take a lot to get through that to where they can begin to receive truth.

The only thing that will get through the wall they have built is love and acceptance from your group. You should forget about trying to

---

* There are many ways for a church to reach out to people besides through ongoing 12-Step meetings. Grace Walk Recovery Ministry is available to assist you. Please contact our office (see information on page 199).

convince them of truth in the early going—and really, at any time—because you never will. We can't fix ourselves or anyone else. But if you love and accept them they will be in a better place for God to reveal the truth that sets free. When people who are struggling first show up, they are not in a place where they can receive anything. So don't just tell them they are loved and accepted. Demonstrate it to them.

Make it a point to let everyone who shows up know that they are accepted regardless of who they are, what they are doing, or where they have been. This is really what we are all looking for. People don't show up at bars night after night just because of the alcohol. That is a draw, but primarily what they are looking for is acceptance. Mike received this e-mail comment from someone who directed a recovery ministry:

> I find that the sharing groups of the 12 Steps brings many closer to another human being in a way that church groups do not. We would never talk about these problems in our own church.

This was my response to her:

> You have brought up a very significant issue. I'm convinced it is the reason for any success that AA has. But I do not believe that 12-Step groups bring people closer than church groups can. I know that is true in many cases, but are we saying that people are more accepted and safer in Alcoholics Anonymous than they are in the church? Perhaps that is true in many churches, but not in the church where people see Jesus' words in action: "By this all men will know that you are my disciples, if you love one another" (John 13:35).
>
> I am convinced that people don't feel safe and accepted only because a church doesn't understand grace and extend it to others. The reason they would never talk about these problems in their own church is because they are rejected and looked down on because of their behavior. You cannot have a ministry to anyone unless they know they are accepted just as they are. It will be very difficult to have a recovery ministry in a church that tends to be legalistic.

Those struggling with addictive behavior go to meetings because they know they will be accepted. If AA can provide a place of acceptance for those who are down and out, how much more should we as Christians be able to do that? Is the church of Jesus Christ so lacking in love that we have to send people to a secular group? Love never fails. Ministry, counseling, sermons, programs fail—but love never fails.

When those struggling with addictive behavior show up, someone should welcome them and make them feel special. Think of the times in your life when someone made you feel that way. Both of us have known a few people in our lives who treated everyone they met as a special person and would give them their undivided attention. They would actually treat each person as someone made in the image of God. Imagine that! Others gravitated to these people. They wanted to be around them and hear from them and learn from them.

You and I may not be blessed with that particular gift but we can extend the love of Christ to people. We can "accept one another...just as Christ accepted you, in order to bring praise to God" (Romans 15:7). If we do this we will have an opportunity to speak the truth in love to them. This is what true ministry is.

Keep in mind that you are not accepting their bad behavior or even their beliefs—you are accepting them as God accepts you, which is just as you are. As *The Message* paraphrases it,

> Welcome with open arms fellow believers who don't see things the way you do. And don't jump all over them every time they do or say something you don't agree with—even when it seems that they are strong on opinions but weak in the faith department. Remember, they have their own history to deal with. Treat them gently (Romans 14:1).

Anyone with an addictive behavior has a history of experiencing rejection and condemnation. God tells us there is no more condemnation. He doesn't reject and condemn them, so let us make sure we don't. Remember, don't judge people and tell them what they're doing wrong. Don't tell them what to do. Our ministry is not to judge people, make them do right, or fix them.

You will have people show up who may not know Christ. And even if they do, they may be so spiritually bound and emotionally traumatized that they are unable to receive any truth. They may be very resistant and even argumentative. How do you respond to a person like this? As we have noted earlier in the book, "From now on we regard no one from a worldly point of view. Though we once regarded Christ in this way, we do so no longer" (2 Corinthians 5:16). My (Mike's) pastor, Herb Sims, says this is the way to love people, and both of us believe he is right. It can be done only with the love of God, which resides in you. You will not be able to forgive except through His life (Spirit) in you, and you can only truly love and accept others by faith.

What to Expect

As you love, accept, and support people who are struggling, don't expect them to be consistent and follow though, because they won't. Realize where they are coming from and all the baggage they are carrying. If people could stop doing what they know they should stop, and start doing what they know they should do, they would not be addicted—and we would not need to have a recovery ministry. Remember we are accepting the person as they are, not their behavior.

Realize that this is a niche ministry. Addictive behavior carries a stigma. Don't expect people with a problem to flock to your meetings. Expect your recovery ministry to have fits and starts and be slow going, especially in the beginning. Keep in mind, though, that your purpose is not to attract great numbers, but to minister the truth that sets people free. The only people who can receive this truth are people God is working on and bringing to a point where they can receive it. Remember that this is His ministry.

Although we do know the truth and have the answer in Jesus, some people will not be able to receive it, because they are not in a place of desperation and haven't come to the end of self and their resources. They haven't been disabused of the notion that they can do something to deal with their problem. They are looking for a program to tell them what to do, and when they find out you don't have that program they will look elsewhere. That is fine, and there are countless programs that will tell them what to do. They actually need to try everything they can in order to find out that nothing works and only Christ can set them free.

A man struggling with addictive behavior had attended a 12-Step group some years before, but he was thoroughly turned off because they just talked about their problem and their failures. This is really the problem with most support groups (secular or Christian). The truth is that most people struggling with addictive behaviors know more about the problem than they would like to, but they have no clue about the answer. I (Mike) attended hundreds of AA meetings years ago, and I realized they knew more about the problem than most pastors and counselors do, but nothing about the answer.

You can relax and watch what God is doing as you participate with Him in setting captives free.

Some will come back when they find that no program, principles, steps, methods, or any other thing can set them free, but a Person can. The timing is God's, and unless the Holy Spirit reveals the truth to them, they don't know it. Many have the information or knowledge, but until God reveals truth to them, it is just that—information. Your ministry is to be available to love and accept them and tell them the truth and point them to Jesus. If you understand this it takes the burden off you to accomplish anything. You can relax and watch what God is doing as you participate with Him in setting captives free.

We can guarantee you that you will go through discouragement and disappointment. It happens with any ministry, but particularly recovery ministry. That is why you need to be sure that God has called you to this. If you are sure, then you will be able to get through the discouragement that will surely come. We're simply being realistic. I (Mike) would not have chosen this ministry, but I knew God had called me to it. So over the last 27 years I have chosen to stay in it, though there have been times of discouragement and disappointment. But what else could I do? This is where I find contentment and fulfillment. You will too—and there is great joy in seeing a person come out of bondage into God's glorious light and freedom.

It makes it all worthwhile to see a child of God understand who he is in Christ and find his freedom from addictive behavior. This is what Jesus came for, and now He allows us to participate with Him in revealing to people who they are and what they have in Him.

Spreading the Word

When you start a ministry a key question to ask is, "Who do we want to reach?" I believe Scripture gives us a clear answer in a passage we have looked at earlier in this book. Isaiah 61:1 says this:

> The Spirit of the Sovereign LORD is on me, because the LORD has anointed me to proclaim good news to the poor. He has sent me to bind up the brokenhearted, to proclaim freedom for the captives and release from darkness for the prisoners.

In Luke 4:18 Jesus tells us He is the fulfillment of that Scripture. This is what He came for; this is what true ministry is: It is to reach out to the brokenhearted, who are in bondage and darkness, and point them to Him.

Remember what Oswald Chambers said: "The only valid ministry is to point people to Christ." We are not saying that there are not many practical and reasonable things that can be done, but if we really want to help such people we must point them to the One who can set them free. Most of these people do not attend church. Many are Christians, but they have been struggling with the bondage of addiction so long they have given up on the church. Whether they are Christians or not, they are brokenhearted and in bondage, and they need the One who can free them.

We need to reach out to those outside the church. For that reason a church building may not be the ideal place to meet. Nonetheless, in most cases that will be the best place, especially if you are conducting a recovery ministry under its auspices. We will keep repeating this, but it is so important—you must have the support of the leadership of the church to conduct such a ministry there. If you do have the support and a team of trained and competent people with a passion, it will be almost impossible to not have an effective ministry.

After the ministry is up and going, and people are finding their freedom in Christ, they will spread the word. Word of mouth is the best advertising available. We believe most churches are missing what might be the best outreach program available—reaching out to those struggling with the bondage of addiction. Many churches would respond that they have tried to reach those outside the church, but with very little results. That is true, but in most cases their goal was to get people to come. In order to reach people you need to touch a "felt need," and most of them do not feel a need to go to church. Many in the bondage of addiction have tried it and found it didn't meet their "felt need."

However, most of those struggling with addictive behavior have a "felt need" to get out of the bondage and darkness in which they are trapped. Many have attended AA and other 12-Step programs with little result. In the last 25 years we have talked to countless people who have not found freedom in a 12-Step program. A lot of them have gone through many treatment centers, both secular and Christian, and not found any answer. What you will be offering them is different: It's not a way to cope, such as going to meetings and so on the rest of their lives, but an answer: true and lasting freedom in Christ. As we pointed out, the most successful advertising is word of mouth. You can't argue with a satisfied customer, as they say.

There are ways to get the word out that are not cost-prohibitive. If the church supports the recovery ministry (and this shouldn't be an option), they can do it through bulletins, pulpit announcements, their website, and other ways. Hopefully the church will be willing to supply some funding, with which you could print brochures or flyers. Grace Walk Recovery Ministry will list your recovery ministry on our website. Some Christian radio stations will let you provide announcements about your weekly meetings. Some recovery ministries have purchased mailing lists and set up mailings in their area. Though you may not have the funds to do much of this, we are still convinced you will have a successful outreach to the community as people are encouraged, helped, and find freedom in Christ.

Conclusion

Living in the Freedom Christ Has Provided

Summing up the truth and reality of who you are and what you have in Christ

We (Steve and Mike) have been Christians for a combined total of about 80 years. Through all of these years, the question that has sooner or later surfaced in the overwhelming majority of conversations and discussions among Christians has been this: "How do we live the abundant, victorious life?" or some variant of it, such as "How do I get free?"

But maybe when we ask "How?" we are asking the wrong question. As we noted at the beginning of this book, *how* is defined as "in what manner or way; by what means; a manner or method of doing something." There is no formula, program, method, or way, no principles or steps, to live the Christian life—to get free or be sanctified. The reason is because now "it is finished!" It has all been done. There is nothing that we need to do or can do. So long as we search for the "how" to get free, shape up, get our act together—you name it—it results in futility, frustration, and failure. We are showing we believe the lie that we can free or sanctify ourselves. And again, what happens? Lies keep us in bondage, but truth sets us free.

The Key Truth of Abiding in Christ

We're confident that most Christians would agree that if we could abide in Christ we would be walking by faith, avoiding sin, and trusting Him as our life in our responses and actions. If we could abide in Him, we could do what's right, stop our destructive behavior, cease damaging our relationships, stay out of trouble, and experience peace, joy, and freedom. But the question comes up again: *How? How* do we abide in Christ?

The word *abide* means "to stay, remain, and be."* Could it possibly be as simple as just to be who I am? *Yes, it could.* Who are you? That is the crucial issue. Who do you think you are? Do you believe that you are an alcoholic, an addict, or a codependent? Do you believe you are an anorexic, a perfectionist, a workaholic? We have said throughout this book, if you believe you are any one of these things then you will act accordingly. *But* if you know that in Christ you are righteous, holy, blameless, dead to sin, freed from it, and perfect and complete in Him, you don't have to spend most of your time and effort trying to shape up. Jesus does not say to "abide *with* Me," but to "abide *in* Me." We can do this because that is where we now are and where we are going to be for all eternity.

One great problem is that we often see the words "abide in Me" as a command to do something, to attain a goal. But we are *already* in Him. Nothing can take us out of Him. He is in us. Nothing in this world or any other can take us out of Him. All we have to do is stay there, remain there, live there. In other words, we don't have to do anything except believe the truth that we are freed from sin and live in the reality that we are in Christ and He is in us.

Stay Out of Fantasy

What about when we walk after the flesh and live like the devil? We have believed a lie and moved into deception. That's the only real weapon Satan has against us, and if he can get us to believe a lie he can jerk us around like a bulldog does a rag doll. But have we actually left Christ? No. We haven't even wandered away. We have just been deceived. So what we do to get back to abiding in Him? *Nothing!* Rather, we again realize the truth of who we are and where we are. Abiding in

---

* *Abide* is the Greek word *meno*, defined in *Strong's Dictionary* as "to stay (in a given place, state, relation or expectancy)—abide, continue, dwell, endure, be present, remain."

Him is simply recognizing that we *do* abide in Him! We can simply thank Him that we are in Him, abiding in Him, and He in us.

I told her, "You don't have to give in to that."...
The only real power Satan has over us is the
lie, but she believed she couldn't resist it.

Now, couldn't we call Satan's lie a fantasy? Most people seem to have no clue as to how dangerous it is to indulge in fantasy. There are a lot of messed-up people today because they have spent so much time outside of reality. The truth is, in many ways the mind cannot distinguish between what is real and what is not. Although you are not what you think you are, what you think is how you will act. Your behavior will always be a result of what you are thinking.

One time I (Mike) was leading a young woman through "The Steps to Freedom in Christ" (a process of confession and repentance). She was demonized, and I made the mistake of confronting the demonic prematurely. She let out a shrill, inhuman scream. After she calmed down and got under control, I said to her, "You knew that was coming, didn't you?" and she replied she did. I then told her, "You don't have to give in to that." Of course she didn't. The only real power Satan has over us is the lie, but she believed she couldn't resist it. A few hours later, when this young woman walked out the door, free in Christ, she said to me, "No one has ever told me I don't have to give in to that."

Escaping Unreality

Every person who has ever struggled with an addictive behavior has felt the same overpowering urges. We believed the lie behind the temptation—that it was so powerful we couldn't overcome it—and gave in to it. But 1 Corinthians 10:13 says,

> No temptation has overtaken you but such as is common to man; and God is faithful, who will not allow you to be tempted beyond what you are able, but with the

temptation will provide the way of escape also, so that you will be able to endure it (NASB).

The way of escape is not out the back door. It is at the threshold of our mind before the temptation or thought enters and settles down to stay. It may have been Martin Luther who first said, "You can't stop the birds from flying over your head, but you can keep them from building a nest in your hair."

We will know most thoughts that are not in line with the truth for what they are. They will be such things as accusations, condemnations, and sinful inclinations. We should just ignore them and not give them place. We must remember that no negative, accusing, condemning, or tempting thought comes from God. Sometimes we will experience what seems to be overpowering urges and it will be necessary to follow the advice of 1 Peter 5:7-9: "Be of sober spirit, be on the alert. Your adversary, the devil, prowls around like a roaring lion, seeking someone to devour. But resist him, firm in your faith" (NASB).

God tells us exactly what we need to do. "Submit yourselves, then, to God. Resist the devil, and he will flee from you" (James 4:7). And Philippians 4:6-8 tells us what to do to experience God's peace:

> Do not be anxious about anything, but in every situation, by prayer and petition, with thanksgiving, present your requests to God. And the peace of God, which transcends all understanding, will guard your hearts and your minds in Christ Jesus. Finally, brothers and sisters, whatever is true, whatever is noble, whatever is right, whatever is pure, whatever is lovely, whatever is admirable—if anything is excellent or praiseworthy—think about such things.

Staying Where You've Been Put

What has God called us to do? Nothing more than to live in the truth that we are in Jesus and He is in us. We can stay where God has placed us—"in Christ." We can remain where we are—"in Christ" and not move into deception. We can *be* who we *are*—"the righteousness of God in Him."

Someone once asked Herb Sims, the pastor of Grace Life Church, "How do we practice the righteousness of God?" "Breathe," he answered. Isn't that an audacious statement? Yes—but how audacious is the declaration in Hebrews 10:14: "By one sacrifice he has made perfect forever those who are being made holy"? If we are going to live in the freedom that has been provided for us we are going to have to realize that what Christ has accomplished for us is not simply audacious, but miraculous and supernatural.

I (Mike) have experienced the freedom of simply believing God. When Julia, my wife, and I moved to Atlanta in 1991, we were unable to sell our house in Birmingham, Alabama, for anywhere near as much as we'd hoped. We got only a small amount of our equity. I had been free from my addiction for only a little over two years, and my credit rating was not very good, so we couldn't get a mortgage on the house we leased in Atlanta.

After a year we applied for a mortgage. The lenders told us, "We can't give you a mortgage—you have a judgment against you." The judgment was eight years old, and I hadn't been aware of it. The original amount had been compounding interest, and it was so high after eight years that we could never have settled it. As we walked out of the mortgage office I was crestfallen. We really had nothing, and what little money we had we'd put into the house on which we couldn't get a mortgage. Julia turned to me and said, "I kept looking at the picture on the wall in the office—*The Last Journey of the U.S.S. Victory*, and thinking 'victory.'" That wasn't what I was thinking, but on the way back to my office God spoke to me and said, "I have given you the victory—are you going to believe Me?"

"Yes, Lord," I answered. "I believe You. Thank You." And I really didn't worry about it after that. We ended up being able to pay off the judgment for a small percentage of what it was, and got a mortgage on the house at the lowest rate that had been offered in years. But I know and realize that I experienced the victory on the day God said He had given it to me and I had believed Him. "Thanks be to God, who gives us the victory through our Lord Jesus Christ" (1 Corinthians 15:57 NASB).

Just Be Who You Are

God is telling us in the Bible to simply be who we are. Too many Christians read it with a legalistic mindset. They see everything that He tells them to do as a harsh command that is extremely difficult to carry out. However, as we realize who we are and what we have, we understand that "this is the love of God, that we keep His commandments; and His commandments are not burdensome" (1 John 5:3 NASB). We keep His commandments as we abide in Him and He abides in us. Truthfully, we don't really keep them as such, but trust Christ in us to keep them:

> The one who keeps His commandments abides in Him, and He in him. We know by this that He abides in us, by the Spirit whom He has given us (1 John 3:24 NASB).

Jesus tells us similarly, "If you abide in My word, you are My disciples indeed. And you shall know the truth, and the truth shall make you free" (John 8:31-32 NKJV). We are in Christ and we do know truth, so what do we need to do to be free? Simply live in that truth and reality.

So what should our response to all this be? It could be, "Lord, I don't really feel like it, look like it, or act like this, but I thank You that it is true. I thank You and praise You that You have done it all and there is nothing left for me to do. Thank You that I am abiding in Christ and His love, and He is abiding in me. I trust You, depend on You, and rely on You and Your life in me, which is my life. I believe that truth is what You say regardless of my feelings or actions. I determine to know nothing except Jesus Christ and Him crucified. I worship You." As a famous theologian put it, "Do not seek for anything; do not perform anything; do not intend anything. *Simply accept the fact that you are accepted!*"*

—

---

* Paul Tillich, *The Shaking of the Foundations* (New York: Charles Scribner's Sons, 1955), ch. 19, as found at www.religion-online.org/showchapter.asp?title=378&C=84.

As we come to the end of this book, we want to say a particular word to those of you who have a loved one or friend struggling with addictive behavior or are yourself struggling. You can be assured that your heavenly Father cares about you and about your friend or loved one. Dealing with those who are addicted can be mentally, emotionally, and physically draining. Sometimes the situation may even challenge our faith. We may wonder if it really is true that God cares. We may ask, if He does care, why won't He do something about the situation?

There are times in life when we must return to the basics of our faith. Is there a God? Is He loving and good? Is He in control over everything in this world? Although your emotions may not affirm the positive answer to these questions, deep inside yourself you know the truth. The reason you know the truth is because of the Truth (Jesus) who lives inside you, quietly assuring you in the darkest moments that the circumstances you and your loved ones face are outside neither His awareness nor His concern.

> We can rest in confidence that even in the worst times, we are all encompassed and upheld by the enduring love of God.

Keep your eyes on Him. The goal of this book is first and foremost to point you to your heavenly Father as *the* Source of Hope in your life. We have given specific suggestions and instructions about how you can reach out to help those who are addicted, but there are no guidelines that are fail-safe. However, there is One whose love and care are always dependable. Our prayer is that He will work through the things you've learned from this book so you can help, encourage, and accept those who are hurting as they futilely seek to have their needs met through addiction.

Both of us know what is it to experience the ups and downs of dealing with addiction. One of us has experienced it firsthand, and the other has seen it up close and personal in the lives of people he has loved. Ministry to hurting people is never an exact science. There is no formula, steps, or guidelines that guarantee freedom to anybody, but we can rest in confidence that even in the worst times, we are all encompassed and upheld by the enduring love of the God who will never abandon us, never lose passion for us, and never give up on us. Not ever. In all the uncertainties of this life, we may rest in the certainty of His never-ending love.

A Final Encouragement

Writing a book about helping people find freedom from addiction is a daunting task. In this world, the problem of addiction is all-pervasive—it finds its roots in culture from the beginning of mankind's story. For the two of us to suggest to you that we offer the cure for addictive behavior might seem brash and presumptive, but we don't think so. We believe Jesus was speaking literally when He said, "If the Son sets you free, you will be free indeed."

My (Mike's) long struggle with alcohol testifies to the reality that a spiritual cure is the only lasting cure for addiction—or for that matter, any sins in which we may find ourselves involved. After I had tried everything I could find, it was finally by understanding my authentic identity and the power of the indwelling Christ that I have lived in freedom from addiction all these years.

A woman once came to me (Steve) after I had spoken at a conference and told me, "I heard you share this message last year, and I was set free by understanding who I am in Christ. I went back the next week to my group meeting and told them, 'I am not an alcoholic by nature! I am a righteous child of God who has a physical and psychological vulnerability toward alcohol abuse, but that isn't what defines me. I am God's child, created in Christ's image! My name is Nora, and I'm a saint!'"

This kind of understanding is the bull's-eye we are aiming at when we share with people that it is Jesus Christ and Him alone who can truly set them free from their addictions. Programs that leave Him out of the equation are excluding the only hope any of us have for lasting freedom in any area of our lives. Christ, and Christ alone, is our hope.

Perhaps we've written some things in these chapters that have caused you to question our perspective. Maybe you've even strongly disagreed about some of the things we've said. Possibly you have found yourself feeling defensive about some of our observations concerning rehabilitation programs that are built entirely on steps to be followed and meetings to be attended.

Our purpose hasn't been to deny or even diminish the value of the help anybody has received from any source. Our God can and does use anything He wants in order to work in the lives of those He loves. What we've wanted to make clear is that unless the living Christ expresses Himself to us, in us, and then through us, there can be no lasting recovery. The way of Jesus isn't one of rehabilitation or even recovery, but instead *resurrection.*

It is only when we realize that we are dead in terms of having any ability to help ourselves that God is able to step into our situation and raise us up by Divine Life. There may be programs that can "put out the fire" of addiction for a time, sometimes even for a long time, but only the grace of God expressed through Jesus Christ can rebuild the burned-down house that is our broken lives.

A person's goal may be to get free from their addiction. God's goal is far greater. His desire is that they might experience *real* life and know it in the fullest sense of the word (see John 10:10). That is our desire for you too and for those you seek to help find freedom from addiction.

Freedom through Jesus Christ—that is the inheritance of every one of us. To help people find lasting freedom from addiction is to help them find Him. Our prayer is that He may be the resting place for those you want to help—and for you—because there is no true freedom to be found anywhere else.

Format for Freedom

*How to Have a Ministry
Where People Find True and
Lasting Freedom in Christ*

Setting Up a Ministry, Part 1

Presenting the right content

I t is absolutely essential that we realize whatever form the ministry takes, it is just the structure in which we do ministry. Whether you are meeting in a church or a home, and when and where you meet, will not determine whether people find their freedom. You can have the best-organized and well-structured ministry there is, but if you don't present the truth and point them to Jesus, it will be difficult at best for people to find freedom.

There are many recovery ministries with programs that are well-organized. They have excellent content and very practical steps for people to take. However, the crucial issue is, are they being presented with Jesus, the truth that will set them free? Deception is what keeps us from experiencing freedom. That's why a recovery ministry should clearly present the fact that the finished work of Christ has provided each Christian everything a person needs to be free.

We are not convinced that regular weekly meetings are the only or even the best way to minister the truth to those struggling with addictive behavior. For one thing it can place the focus on the person who attends the meeting, rather than on Jesus and His truth. The primary emphasis of most recovery meetings, as we've said previously, is on following their program. The upshot is that the focus is on self and what you should and shouldn't do. That is a surefire prescription for disaster and a recipe for continued bondage.

If you have come to believe that people need at least a weekly meeting, in the next book section we'll present three kinds of meetings you can incorporate into your ministry. As you look over the information, you might think that they are more like discipleship meetings. You would be right. Every Christian needs to be presented with the truth that sets people free so they may grow in grace and be sanctified by faith. A person struggling with an addictive behavior such as alcohol, sex, or drugs is no different than a Christian who is struggling with gossip, materialism, or workaholism.

Keep the Focus on God's Grace

Some Christian recovery groups do a much better job of presenting the truth than do others, but very often something is still missing. One time I (Mike) attended a recovery conference at a church. They did a great job of making it clear that only Jesus could set you free from addiction. They even made it clear that Christians are not alcoholics or addicts by nature, but their identity is that of children of God. However, the focus of the program was on what someone should avoid or do to attain and maintain freedom in Christ.

What was missing in this program and is missing in most of the Christian programs that don't use the 12 Steps and strive to be biblical and Christ-centered is this: As a result of Christ's finished work on the cross, freedom has already been provided for us. It is not something to achieve, but to believe and receive. What is missing is grace.

Usually all of the things such programs tell you to do are excellent, but the problem is they put the cart before the horse. Unless a person has appropriated their identity in Christ, knows the truth that sets free, and has an understanding of grace, *they cannot do these good things on a consistent basis.* All the good things that we attempt without trusting Christ as our life are doomed to failure. When people are unable to follow through, they feel alienated and under condemnation and the vicious cycle of bondage and addiction continues.

When people try to observe regulations and rules, it means they have lost connection with Jesus. Paul says they "are not connected to Christ, the head…These rules may seem wise because they require strong devotion, pious self-denial, and severe bodily discipline. But they provide no help in conquering a person's evil desires" (Colossians 2:19,23 NLT). If you have lost connection with Christ, it really doesn't matter what you are doing. It is an empty pursuit that can only end in despair.

What then do we need to emphasize to really help people get out of the bondage of addiction? Drawing from what we've discussed in earlier chapters, let's begin with the reasons Christians are not free, so we can see what we're up against.

The Top Ten Reasons Christians Are Not Free from Addiction

1. *They have not come to brokenness.* They haven't come to the end of self and still have some confidence in their own resources and abilities. A good indication of this is when they say, "Tell me what to do!" They still believe there is something they can do to sanctify or free themselves.

2. *They have issues of unforgiveness.* This is the number-one way Satan robs us of our freedom. Most Christians in bondage have unresolved anger. Forgiveness is God's only way to deal with it. Unforgiveness equals bondage (see Ephesians 4:26-27).

3. *They do not accept themselves the way they are.* They need to realize that God accepts them just the way they are, and forgive themselves and accept themselves.

4. *They insist on trying to get their feelings to line up with the truth.* This will never happen, because we experience freedom when we live by faith in the truth, regardless of our feelings.

5. *They fail to distinguish between the flesh and their real self.* The flesh constantly wars against the Spirit, but the flesh is *not* who we are. We are not alcoholics, addicts, perfectionists, anorexics, and the like. We are not sinners—we are righteous saints. However, many Christians have no clue that they are dead to sin and freed from it.

6. *They have an inadequate understanding of grace.* They do not understand that as a result of Christ's finished work on the cross there is nothing more for them to do. They do not know they are dead to the law, and they are still trying to perform and measure up so they can feel accepted and worthy, and so they can perfect themselves and find freedom.

7. *They have a wrong concept of God.* They don't know that God accepts them as they are. He has not changed and does not change as a result of their sin. They believe their failure can overcome His grace.

8. *They have never appropriated the truth of their identity in Christ.* It is just information to them, or they are still holding on to a false identity in the flesh. They believe who they are is determined by what they do, instead of by what God says about them.

9. *They have not learned to resist Satan.* They do not understand spiritual warfare—especially Satan's defeat at the cross and their position and authority in Christ. They don't understand that the devil's only weapon against them is the lie. They don't understand that "greater is He who is in you than he who is in the world" and that God has given us the victory through our Lord Jesus Christ.

10. *They don't understand that they have everything that they need, and that they are dead to sin and freed from it.* They still believe that even though Christ is their life and lives in

them, it is up to them to do the right thing, avoid sin, and abstain from wrong behavior. They may know they are saved by faith, but they believe it is up to them to do their best to live the Christian life.

⸙

The basics of recovery to freedom in Christ are, in general, the opposite of what keeps people in bondage:

The Basics of Recovery from Addiction to Freedom in Christ

1. *Give up on self and its resources.*

   - It's not what someone does but what God has done.

   - Everything else is just information until a person comes to the end of themselves and their resources—brokenness.

2. *Submit to God—give up rights, expectations, self, agenda, everything.*

   - Most people have not given up on their agendas, goals, and so on.

   - They must give up their rights to have good things—job, spouse, ministry, and so on.

   - They must give up on their theology and what they have been taught to do to live the Christian life.

3. *They must realize they are dead to the power of sin and that Satan has absolutely no power over them.*

   - Most Christians are fighting battles that have already been won by Christ.

   - The problem is not that they need to change, choose, do something, get somewhere, or get something, but that they need to know and believe that they are dead to sin, alive to God, and complete in Christ.

4. *There is no more condemnation, guilt, shame, and punishment.*

   • They are not products of their past, but of the cross.

   • What are they most aware of when they fail—God's grace and deliverance, or their failure?

   • They must realize that their failure cannot overcome God's grace.

   • They must realize that truth is still true and God is still God, even when they fail.

5. *Because of their co-crucifixion, the old person they were died with Christ.*

   • Knowing that the old sin-loving sinner they used to be is dead and no more is truth that sets free and keeps them free.

   • This is the key that enables them to appropriate their identity.

6. *They need a true concept of God.*

   • They can't come to Him and bond with Him without it.

   • They will not come to God until they know He accepts them just as they are and nothing they do can make Him love them more, and nothing they do can make Him love them less.

   • They need to know that "the only lasting freedom from self-consciousness comes from a profound aware-ness that God loves me as I am and not as I should be" (Brennan Manning).

7. *They must know that they are not under law, but under grace.*

   • If they don't know they're dead to the law, they will be trying to perform and measure up.

   • An understanding of grace is the only thing that

will get them off the performance-based acceptance treadmill.

- They understand they are free from sin when they understand they are not under law, but under grace (Romans 6:14).

8. *They need to walk in truth regardless of their feelings or circumstances.*

- The key to the victorious Christian life is acting on the truth.

- They need to do this regardless of their feelings.

9. *They must realize they are not a victim, but a victor.*

- They need to know their position in Christ.

- They are seated with Christ in the heavenly places.

- They have been given the victory and are conquerors.

10. *They must believe that as a result of the finished work of Christ they are freed from the power of sin.*

- Christ is in them and they are in Him; they have everything they need for life and godliness.

If a person believes he is an addict then he has no option but to spend the rest of his life engaging in addictive behavior or living his life trying not to.

The Indispensable Foundation: Identity

We must emphasize again that at the core of the program—so basic and foundational that if we neglect it the rest of what we do will not work—is identity in Christ. What do we mean by this? Briefly, it is to know that your old sin-loving self was crucified and is dead and buried. It is no more. It is to know that you are dead to sin and freed from it. You are a righteous, holy saint. That is your true identity. It is to know that you haven't merely been improved or made better—and because you're God's child and have the Holy Spirit you can now do right. Christ in you is your life and who you are.

Our true identity is what most Christian recovery programs do not teach. This is not surprising. As we have said, most programs (both Christian and secular) believe and stress that the person is an alcoholic or addict, even though they are a new creation in Christ. Many programs have the person confess they are an addict or alcoholic at every meeting. The movie actor Corey Haim died in 2010 in a drug-related episode at 38 years old. He had tried many different things to get free of his addiction, but in a 2007 interview, Haim called himself "a chronic relapser for the rest of my life." Almost without exception, all who are struggling with an addictive behavior believe this. After his film roles dried up, Haim tried to auction his extracted teeth and locks of his hair on the Internet. At the time of his death his assets included a few thousand dollars in cash, some clothing, and royalty rights.

I (Mike) recently received an e-mail from a man whose 26-year-old son was in his second treatment center for addiction to prescription drugs. The man said his son was becoming somewhat depressed in the rehab clinic over the thought that his disease was not curable and that the rest of his life would be consumed with sponsors, meetings, and working the 12-Step program. The father said his son was feeling that, whereas his past had been obsessed with taking drugs, in the future his life would be equally obsessed with "not taking drugs."

We think this young man has it figured out. If a person believes he is an addict then he has no option but to spend the rest of his life engaging in addictive behavior or living his life trying not to. However, those who have experienced their freedom understand who they are and what they have. They don't return to their old lifestyle of bondage, whether that bondage is engaging in or trying to avoid their addictive behavior.

Perhaps you are thinking that it's really a tall order to present all of the truths we just listed to people seeking freedom. It's really not.

The main thing it requires is a mindset to believe that freedom is not something to attain, but has already been given to you. As you believe that, you will be able to communicate the truth that sets free to others. You will be able to have a ministry that sees people released and restored.

Setting Up a
Ministry, Part 2

Formats and resources

W e are convinced that only as we clearly present the truth that sets free does any person have a chance to find freedom. Our prime reason for writing this book is to do whatever we can to help you and anyone who has a heart and a passion for ministering to those in the bondage of addiction. As we look at the addiction epidemic in our world today and see so few getting real help, our hearts are heavy, and we want to make our resources and ourselves available to you. We know that we have an answer, and His name is Jesus. We want to give you all the information, help, and resources you need to point people to Jesus and the truth that sets you free.

If you would like to have a recovery meeting or ministry and present the truth that sets free, there are several ways that you can do this, which we will give in detail shortly. We also want to mention that I (Mike) am available to come to your church and conduct a Freedom from Addictive Behaviors Conference and a Recovery Ministry Leadership Training Seminar. However, if this is not possible, the training can be done through DVDs and webinars.*

---

* The conference is available for a reasonable price on DVDs and includes a 43-page conference manual. The leadership seminar (the Freedom from Addictive Behaviors Advanced Webinar) is conducted on the Internet. The webinar is free, and the only cost is the book and workbook that are used. During the webinar we are available to answer your questions and give you the information and encouragement you need. There is also a Freedom from Addictive Behaviors Basic Webinar that is presented twice a year.

Gathering a Team

As you go about setting up a recovery ministry, the most crucial requirement is to have the right people. We strongly advise you not to go it alone. If you don't have a team of people who are committed and trained there is little possibility of success.

How many do you need in your team? That primarily depends on the size of your church and your contacts, if you are doing your ministry through a church. You and one other would be a good place to start. Perhaps you know a person or two who share your interest in ministering to those struggling with addictive behavior. The key is to begin it with a few people who have a passion for it and are trained. Does it have to be someone who has struggled with addictive behavior? No, it does not. What you need is someone who knows the truth that sets free. There are people God has given a passion to minister to those with addictive behavior even though they have not struggled with it themselves.

The basic book that clearly presents the truth that sets free is *Freedom from Addiction* by Dr. Neil Anderson and Mike and Julia Quarles. The first seven chapters present my (Mike's) testimony of my struggle with alcoholism, the many things I tried to get free, and how I finally found the truth. We encourage everyone to read this book, as it is a comprehensive presentation of the truth that sets free. Each group leader should have attended a Freedom from Addictive Behaviors Conference, watched the conference DVDs, or attended the Freedom from Addictive Behaviors Basic Webinar (which is an abbreviated form of the conference). They should also have gone through the Freedom from Addictive Behaviors Advanced Webinar, which will take them through *Freedom from Addiction* and the *Freedom from Addiction Workbook*.

As mentioned, our ministry stands ready to help you in whatever way we can, either in person or online. Our Freedom from Addictive Behaviors Basic Webinar lasts six weeks, and our Freedom from Addictive Behaviors Advanced Webinar lasts ten weeks. Both are offered twice a year at no charge. Once some people are trained and you have the support of the leadership of the church, then you can promote and begin a recovery ministry.*

Where to Meet

Where you should meet really depends on what is available. If you have the full support of the leadership of your church and are operating the ministry under its auspices it will work fine to meet in the church building. But if you decide to have it in a neutral place such as a school, office building, home, and so on that can also work well. There is absolutely nothing wrong with meeting in a home, and it has the advantage of being a place in which people can feel especially welcomed and accepted.

——❧——

Here are some tips and an overview of the resources you can use to present the truth that sets free in a ministry, whether it's a weekly meeting, one on one, or in some other format. Fortunately there are lots of excellent resources available.†

How to Conduct a Meeting

Someone should have the responsibility to make sure people, especially newcomers, are welcomed when they come into the place you're meeting. The best way is for your team and other regulars to take turns doing this. (This is a great way to get to know everyone.) If someone who is to do the welcoming is unable to make the meeting, they should call someone else to do it. If no one shows up to do the welcoming, someone else should pick up the ball. Don't let this slide for any reason. For newcomers this will be more important than the truth that is shared during the meeting. You can be certain that almost all of them come with reluctance and apprehension.

The welcoming person should greet the newcomer and give them

---

* We do plan to offer a webinar based on this book, probably in late 2012. Contact our office for more information (see page 199).

† See also "Grace Walk Recovery Resources" in the Resources section that follows in this book.

a brief introduction about the meeting and what is taking place. Have a sign-in sheet with a place for phone numbers and e-mail addresses, and ask them to sign in. If they hesitate, let it go.

At the beginning of the time you should have 15 to 30 minutes to interact so people can get to know each other and newcomers can be informed about what is going on. Also give them a copy of our bookmark, which has "Who I Am in Christ" on one side and "The Overcomer's Covenant in Christ" on the other, as well as the paper with the testimonies of me (Mike) and Julia, my wife.*

If possible, have a book table with recovery resources available for them to purchase.† If you are showing the *Freedom from Addictive Behaviors Conference* DVDs, give the newcomer a copy of the accompanying manual or of the part of the manual your meeting will cover. (The manual can be downloaded from our website.) If you are going through the *One Day at a Time* devotional, have several loaner copies available to use during the meeting. Or at the least, have copies of the devotional portion that will be covered so the newcomer can follow along. Find out a little bit about them, such as what they do and where they are from, and introduce them to as many participants as possible.

Communication is vital, and personal
communication always works best.

After the meeting, ask them what they thought, but don't argue with them. Just say a word of positive testimony about how the meeting helps you and that you hope they will come back. Give them your phone number, and ask them to call you if they have any questions or you can help in any way.

The person who did the welcoming should call all the newcomers during the following week if they have left a phone number. The sign-in sheet can provide the information for a database; everyone should be

---

* An initial supply of bookmarks and testimonies is available at no charge.

† Again, see "Grace Walk Recovery Resources" in the Resources section that follows in this book.

e-mailed weekly to remind them of the upcoming meeting. The message doesn't have to be long, just the invitation and a word of encouragement. Don't delete anyone from the database unless they request it. We have seen people who we haven't heard from in years call us or show up at a meeting. If you will send your database to Grace Walk Recovery Ministry, everyone will receive a newsletter via e-mail from the ministry monthly. Communication is vital, and personal communication always works best.

Using the Recommended Resources

Introductory option: *Grace Walk* book

The book *Grace Walk* (by Steve) is a primer on the Christian's identity in Christ. While it doesn't deal directly with addiction, it has been helpful in introducing many people to the foundational truths that are necessary for living in freedom. The book has 12 chapters, with study/discussion questions for each chapter.

Option 1: Freedom from Addictive Behaviors Conference *DVDs with Discussion Questions*

You could have a weekly meeting for a specified number of weeks (probably 18 to 20) and present the *Freedom from Addictive Behaviors Conference* DVDs. They contain nine messages and a question-and-answer session with me (Mike). For discussion you can use the leader's guide, which has ten discussion questions for each message. It is best if you take two sessions for each of the nine messages, as the material from one message would be difficult to do in one session. The discussion questions give the person an opportunity to digest and deal with the truth that is presented.

This is an excellent way to begin a recovery ministry because the conference DVDs cover all the basics of addiction as well as God's answer. They present the truth and give the participants an opportunity to discuss it. Also, since people tend to be apprehensive at first, they can watch the DVDs and respond to the discussion questions when they are ready.

Although we recommend that the group leader go through the

training (the Freedom from Addictive Behavior Basic and Advanced Webinars), all the leader really has to do is ask the questions after showing the DVD. Remember that it can be slow going to start a weekly meeting and have people participate, because they come in with a lot of baggage and hurt.

If you are operating under the auspices of a church, you could offer a Sunday-school class—or a Sunday-evening or Wednesday-evening class if your church meets at these times.*

Option 2: The One Day at a Time Devotional

The *One Day at a Time* devotional is divided into 12 devotions on each of the ten truths we believe people need to know to be free (see the previous section). So there are 120 devotions in all. Each devotion is two to three pages long, with questions and a place to journal at the end (so no leader's guide is needed). If you want to have something ongoing you can have a weekly meeting and cover four to six devotions a week. If you go through fewer each week, this would be less overwhelming, and participants could keep up even if they missed a meeting here and there. For instance, if you cover three devotions a week, it will take 40 weeks to go through the complete devotional.

The meeting's introduction. We strongly suggest that you begin the meeting with everyone standing and reading out loud together all of the statements on the "Who I Am in Christ" bookmark. This reminds them that they are not addicts and who they are in Christ. The leader can then do a five-to-ten-minute introduction on the topic or topics, although this is not absolutely essential. Someone can give a testimony or share some thoughts on a Bible verse. If no one wants to do a short introduction, someone can read the devotional(s) for that week along with the Bible verses. After this everyone can stand and pray Ephesians 1:16-20 together before they break up into small groups.

Prayer from Ephesians 1:16-20. (Pronouns have been changed so participants will be praying for themselves and the others in the group.)

---

* See "What Grace Walk Recovery Ministry Can Offer" in the Resources section for a list of the topics the conference covers and a brief explanation of them.

> We pray constantly, asking God, the glorious Father of our
> Lord Jesus Christ, to give us spiritual wisdom and under-
> standing, so that we might grow in our knowledge of God.
> We pray that our hearts will be flooded with light so that
> we can understand the wonderful future he has promised
> to those he called. We want to realize what a rich and glo-
> rious inheritance he has given to his people. We pray that
> we will begin to understand the incredible greatness of his
> power for us who believe him. This is the same mighty
> power that raised Christ from the dead and seated him
> in the place of honor at God's right hand in the heavenly
> realms. (Adapted from Ephesians 1:16-20 NLT 1996.)*

Everyone should be given a copy of this prayer. We have used the
New Living Translation as we believe it is easily understood and user-
friendly, but it is up to the leaders as to what version to use.

Small-group discussion and sharing. Following the introduction to
the meeting, you can break up into small groups for discussion and
sharing. In the beginning you will probably just have one group. It
really will not matter if people are struggling with different addictive
behaviors. We know this is not the prevailing opinion and practice, but
it is truth that sets people free, and there are not different versions of the
truth for individual issues. (The same truth that set me—Mike—free
from alcoholism set my wife, Julia, free from codependency.)

As your attendance grows you can divide up into different groups,
but we recommend that each group cover the same basic material.
Some possible group divisions are

- chemically dependent men and women
- codependent men and women
- eating disorders
- adult children of chemically addicted

---

* See also "Prayers to Begin and End Recovery Meetings" in the Resources section.

- recovery from sexual/physical abuse (women)
- sexual addiction (men)

You may never have more than one group. Most likely you will not unless you are in a very large church—and this is fine.

The small group should focus on discussion and sharing. We recommend getting things going by asking for volunteers to read a paragraph aloud in the devotion(s) you are going to discuss. If no one volunteers, the small-group leader can read a paragraph and ask what people think, ask one of the questions at the end of the devotion, or any other that pertains to the topic.

Leaders don't need to have the gift of teaching, because they are leading a discussion and not teaching. However, they should have gone through the training and know the truth that sets free. They need to be able to keep the discussion on track and bring people back to the truth being discussed when need be. We don't want to discourage sharing, but some people will spend all of the time talking about their problem if they are allowed to. The focus should be on the truth that sets free.*

The end of the meeting. After the small groups, it is good to have everyone stand and read out loud together the "Overcomer's Covenant in Christ" on the other side of the bookmark. This reminds them that the focus is not what they do, but what Christ has done, and that they are set free not by how they behave, but by what they believe. Then close the meeting by praying Ephesians 3:16-21 together.

Prayer from Ephesians 3:16-21. (Pronouns have been changed so participants will be praying for themselves and the others in the group.)

I pray that from his glorious, unlimited resources he will give us mighty inner strength through his Holy Spirit. And I pray that Christ will be more and more at home

---

* See "Guidelines for Group Discussion and Sharing" in the Resources section.

in our hearts as we trust in him. May our roots go down deep into the soil of God's marvelous love. And may we have the power to understand, as all God's people should, how wide, how long, how high, and how deep his love really is. May we experience the love of Christ, though it is so great we will never fully understand it. Then we will be filled with the fullness of life and power that comes from God. Now glory be to God! By his mighty power at work within us, he is able to accomplish infinitely more than we would ever dare to ask or hope. May he be given glory in the church and in Christ Jesus forever and ever through endless ages. Amen. (Adapted from Ephesians 3:16-21 NLT 1996). *

Everyone should be given a copy of the "Declaration of Deliverance, Freedom, and Victory in Christ" and be encouraged to recite it aloud at least once a day.† This is a great way for them to remind themselves of who they are in Christ, what He has done for them, and that their freedom in Him has already been provided to them. Remind them that the objective of reading the declaration is not to do something but to remind themselves of the truth.

Keep in mind that the foregoing is just suggestions to get you going. There really is no one best way to do this, and you should see how the group develops and what works best for it. Some groups may be more informal, and some may follow all the suggested procedures. Each group will develop its own structure.

Option 3: The Freedom from Addiction Workshop

The Freedom from Addiction Workshop requires a lot more effort. People actually work through the *Freedom from Addiction Workbook*, which is a 200-page Bible-based study that is very intensive and

---

* See "Prayers to Begin and End Recovery Meetings" in the Resources section. Here again you can use any translation the team thinks is best, but make sure everyone has a copy.

† See the Resources section.

comprehensive. It requires a lot of motivation and effort, but for those who are willing to, we believe it is by far the best resource available.

Those who have gone through the Freedom from Addictive Behaviors Advanced Webinar have been trained to lead this workshop, which consists of eleven sessions with over 300 PowerPoint slides. (The slides are available for purchase.) We recommend that you take at least two sessions for each topic in the workbook. People going through it will be dealing with issues, and there is just too much material in each chapter to cover in one session.

We recommend you begin each session with the *Freedom from Addiction DVD Seminar.* In this video presentation, Dr. Neil Anderson and Mike and Julia Quarles introduce each section of the workbook

Emphasize the importance of having a mentor, but leave it up to the person to make that decision.

As we pointed out, the *Freedom from Addiction Workbook* requires a lot of motivation and effort. It essentially is a process for discipleship. So it really isn't for everyone. Those who might have an interest should be informed of the time and effort it will demand. Before you offer a class that goes through the workbook, it would be best if you could offer a class on the *Freedom from Addictive Behaviors Conference* DVDs, using the discussion questions, and also one that goes through the *One Day at a Time* devotional. That way you will have people prepared to go further in the discipling process.

We recommend that each person have a mentor to encourage them as they go through the workbook discipleship process.* You may not have enough mentors at the start, but it is not necessary that everyone have a mentor at first. In fact it is probably better that they settle in and make sure they want to pursue the workbook study. Many are not ready to deal with their issues, and they show up at the meetings for other reasons and then quit coming. We need to leave the timing up to God.

We suggest that you emphasize the importance of having a mentor, but leave it up to the person to make that decision. It works best when

---

* See "Guidelines for Mentors" in the Resources section.

the person asks someone to be their mentor, but before they pick one they should read "Selecting a Mentor" in the Resources section. Mentors should have gone through the training with the Freedom from Addictive Behaviors Conference (live or on DVDs) and the Freedom from Addictive Behaviors Advanced Webinar.

Suggested Materials for Christian Treatment Centers

One of the best-kept secrets in the recovery ministry is the existence of Christian treatment centers. When I (Mike) reluctantly agreed with my wife that I should leave our house I didn't know what to do or where to go. I happened to read in a magazine about a Christian treatment center, and I ended up going to one.

We have a list of over 50 such centers, and not a week goes by that we do not refer people to them.* We support and encourage them, and we believe we have some excellent resources for these centers to use so they can present the truth that sets free—not just good advice and behavior-modification techniques.

Below is our suggested curriculum, which is based on a 28-week program. However, it can be adjusted to fit in with the center's own program calendar.

Weeks 1–10. *Freedom from Addictive Behaviors Conference* DVDs with manuals and leader's guide.

There are nine messages on the conference DVDs and a question-and-answer session at the end. Each of the messages has ten discussion questions in the leader's guide. Each participant should have a copy of the manual. If the length of your program is shorter than 28 weeks you could cover two sessions a week. This should not pose a problem for any residential center. Or if your program is longer, you could spend two weeks on each message. In fact we think it is best to take two sessions for each message.

---

* For more information, contact our office (see page 199).

Weeks 11–20. *Freedom from Addiction* with *Freedom from Addiction Workbook* and *Freedom from Addiction DVD Seminar.*

The *Freedom from Addiction Workbook* has ten sessions and is very intense and comprehensive. It can easily be adapted so you cover one session every two weeks. If your program length is shorter you could cover two sessions a week, but we would advise you to give the residents plenty of time to work through the workbook as it will require a lot of effort. Along with the workbook there are assignments to read in the book *Freedom from Addiction.* In the *Freedom from Addiction DVD Seminar,* Dr. Neil Anderson and Mike and Julia Quarles give an approximately 15-minute introduction to each section of the workbook.*

Weeks 21–28. *The Grace Walk Experience* workbook and the *Grace Walk* book.

Along with the Grace Walk Conference audios or videos, these are the perfect conclusion and summary of the truth that sets free. You can cover two sessions a week or stretch out each session over two weeks to fit in with your program.

Throughout weeks 1–28. *One Day at a Time* daily devotional.

It would be good for each person to have a copy of the devotional during the time they are residents in the treatment center. The book has 12 devotions for each of the 10 topics that cover the truth that sets free. Each resident can be encouraged to read five devotions a week, which will take him through the book in 24 weeks. If your program is shorter than this, they can take the book with them and continue to go through it. (One center gives each graduate a copy of the devotional to take with them.) You may want to have a meeting once a week and encourage residents to share what they are learning. If counseling is available, counselors can use this as a way to find out where people are and what they are learning and processing.

---

* Victory Home in Tallulah Falls, Georgia, which is directed by Rev. Richard Pletsch, uses this in their program and has had excellent success with it.

If you would like to have training for your staff, we offer the ten-session Freedom from Addictive Behaviors Advanced Webinar online. There is no charge for the webinar other than the purchase of the two books *Freedom from Addiction* and the *Freedom from Addiction Workbook*, which comprise the curriculum for the course. Please contact us if you have any interest.

Resources

The Ultimate Deception

*The lie that we need more than what
Christ accomplished on the cross*

The Lie	The Truth
I need to improve, get better.	I am complete in Christ.
I need to get closer to God.	I am in Christ and He is in me.
I need to fight sin.	I am dead to sin.
I need to try harder.	I need to cease from my works.
I need to study my Bible more.	Christ is my wisdom.
I need to improve my mind.	I have the mind of Christ.
I need to seek God.	Christ is my life.
I need to get my act together.	I am righteous.
I need to do right.	I need to trust Christ in me.
I need to discipline myself.	I need to listen to Christ in me.
I need a program to follow.	I have a Person to follow.
I need to abstain from substances.	I have been redeemed.
I need a treatment center.	I need to fix my eyes on Jesus.
I need to be held accountable for my behavior.	I need to take my thoughts captive to the truth.
I need new friends.	I have a *friend* I can trust.
I am a physical being with a spirit.	I am a spiritual being in a body.
I need to get stronger so I can cope.	The power of Christ rests on me.
Indwelling sin is in me and makes me want to sin.	Sin is in my body, but that is not who I am, and I don't want to sin.
I need to pray more and longer.	Christ in me is the hope of glory.

What Do We Need to Do?

We are complete in Christ, and we don't need to do anything or get anything. We need to believe the truth of who we are in Him and what we have in Him.

This doesn't mean we don't pray, read our Bibles, go to church, and so on. But we understand and know that those things are not what we need. *We have been given everything we need for life and godliness,* and we can choose to believe that *we partake of the divine nature and escape the corruption of the world caused by evil desires* (2 Peter 1:3-4).

We need to believe that *I have been crucified with Christ and I no longer live, but Christ lives in me, and the life I now live, I live by faith in the Son of God who loved me and gave Himself for me* (Galatians 2:20). We need to believe that *Christ is our life* (Colossians 3:4).

Jesus, when asked by His disciples, "What shall we do that we may work the works of God?" said, "*The work of God is this: to believe in the one he has sent*" *(John 6:29).* He also said, *You will know the truth, and the truth will set you free…so if the Son sets you free, you will be free indeed* (John 8:32,36).

What's Wrong with the 12 Steps?

What's wrong with the 12 Steps? Absolutely nothing! Everything they cover is helpful and good. The problem is what they *don't* cover. They don't cover what is necessary for a person to be free, such as....

1. The person of Christ—Christ is our life and He lives in us.
2. The work of Christ—God's only answer is in the cross.
3. Forgiveness—God's only answer for anger.
4. Our identity in Christ as a child of God. We are not addicts.
5. Grace—God's method of dealing with us and what He has done for us.
6. Faith—the only way we receive all that God has done for us.
7. God's unconditional love and acceptance.
8. The role and work of the Holy Spirit.
9. An answer for guilt and condemnation.
10. An understanding that our battle is in the mind and of God's answer for it.
11. Our position in Christ gives us victory over Satan.
12. Spiritual warfare—how to win the battle.
13. Our co-crucifixion with Christ frees us from the power of sin.
14. Being dead to the law frees us from performance-based acceptance.
15. Being dead to the world frees us from demands of others.
16. The role of the flesh (our learned independence).
17. Prayer.
18. The Word of God.

The 12 Steps do not focus on the finished work of Christ as the answer for addictive behavior. They are likely the best program for enabling a person to cope with a problem, but they lack the necessary components to set a person *free* from the problem.

This should not come as a surprise, since freedom is found only through Christ and His finished work on the cross. In Romans 7:24 Paul did not ask, "*What* will set me free?" There is no "what," no program, that will set you free. He asked, "*Who* will set me free?" The answer is, "Thanks be to God through Jesus Christ our Lord!" (Romans 7:25 NASB). As Jesus said, "If the Son sets you free, you will be free indeed" (John 8:36).

Jesus also said, "The truth will set you free" (John 8:32). God doesn't have a different answer for the addict than for anyone else. God doesn't have a separate truth or answer for the addict. The truth that sets people free from alcoholism and drug addiction is the same truth that sets them free from codependency, perfectionism, controlling, materialism, workaholism, and any other manifestation of the flesh. God's answer for addiction is freedom in Christ.

Freedom is the birthright of every child of God. It comes with the package. Every person in Christ has died to sin, is freed from it, and is complete in Christ.

The Finished Work of Christ

It is finished!
You have it all.
There is nothing left to do,
but by faith believe and receive
what Christ has provided for you.

"By one offering He has perfected for
all time those who are sanctified."

—Hebrews 10:14 NASB

1. All your sins are forgiven (Ephesians 4:32; Colossians 2:13;
   1 John 2:12).
2. Satan has been disarmed and defeated (Colossians 2:15).
3. The record of charges against you has been canceled and nailed
   to the cross (Colossians 2:14).
4. The old sin-loving sinner you were has been crucified and is dead
   and buried and gone (Romans 6:4).
5. The old you no longer lives, but Christ lives in you—and you now
   live by the faith of the Son of God, who loved you and gave Himself
   for you (Galatians 2:20).
6. You are dead to sin and alive to God (Romans 6:11).
7. You have been washed, justified, and sanctified and are freed
   from sin (1 Corinthians 6:11; Romans 6:8).
8. You are the temple of God, and the Spirit of God lives in you
   (1 Corinthians 3:16).
9. Christ is your very life, and your life is now hidden with Christ in
   God (Colossians 3:3-4).

10. You are a new creation in Christ—the old has passed away, the new has come (2 Corinthians 5:17).

11. There is no more condemnation, guilt, shame, and punishment (Romans 8:1).

12. The world has been crucified to you, and you have been crucified to the world (Galatians 6:14).

13. You are born again and have overcome the world, and Satan cannot harm you (1 John 5:4).

14. Christ in you is the hope of glory (Colossians 1:27).

15. You are complete in Christ, and He is the head over all rule and authority (Colossians 2:10).

16. Jesus is in the Father—and you are in Jesus, and He is in you (John 14:20).

17. You have died to the law and have been released from it (Romans 7:6).

18. Sin shall not be your master, because you are not under law, but under grace (Romans 6:14).

19. You are the righteousness of God in Christ (2 Corinthians 5:21).

20. Christ in you is your wisdom, righteousness, sanctification, and redemption (1 Corinthians 1:30).

21. You have been sanctified and made perfect forever (Hebrews 10:14).

22. Christ has set you free, and you are free indeed (John 8:36).

23. You have an anointing from God and you know the truth (1 John 2:20).

24. God is for you and will give you all things (Romans 8:31-32).

25. You have been given the victory (1 Corinthians 15:57).

26. You are born of God, and Jesus keeps you safe; the evil one cannot touch you (1 John 5:18).

27. You are from God and overcome evil spirits because greater is He who is in you than He who is in the world (1 John 4:4).

28. You have been called, justified, sanctified, and glorified (Romans 8:30).

29. Jesus is praying for you (Romans 8:34)
30. You have been given everything you need for life and godliness through Christ (2 Peter 1:3).
31. You have been blessed with every spiritual blessing in Christ (Ephesians 1:3).
32. You have been made alive, raised up with Christ, and seated with Him in the heavenly realm, and God has put all things under His feet (Ephesians 1:20-22; 2:6).
33. God has set His seal of ownership on you, putting His Holy Spirit in you to guarantee what is to come (2 Corinthians 1:22).

Nothing can separate you from the love of Christ—not
hardship, persecution, famine, danger, death, demons,
our fears for today, our worries about tomorrow, and even the
powers of hell can't keep God's love away. Nothing in all creation
will be able to separate you from the love of God in Jesus Christ.

—Romans 8:35-39 NLT, adapted

Thirty Things Mike Tried to Get Free from Addictive Behavior

1. A consistent quiet time
2. Bible study
3. Fasting
4. Visitation evangelism
5. Christian 12-Step program
6. Accountability group
7. Hundreds of AA meetings and five different AA sponsors
8. Christian counselors
9. Christian psychiatrist
10. Secular psychiatrist
11. Christian psychologist
12. Secular psychologist
13. Addictions counselor
14. Three-day session with an addictions specialist in New Jersey
15. Secular treatment center
16. Christian treatment center
17. Reading every book on addiction he could find
18. Healing of memories session
19. Baptism of the Spirit session
20. Casting out demons session (twice)
21. Public confession
22. Group therapy
23. Taking the drug Antabuse (and getting ill twice when he drank)
24. Discipline by his church

25. A rigid schedule with every minute planned

26. Hundreds of hours studying scriptural principles

27. Memorizing chapters of Scripture

28. Discipleship groups

29. Prayer

30. Promises to God and his wife

Why didn't any of this work? None of these things were necessarily bad, and some were very good things to do. But they were all things I (Mike) was doing in the flesh, depending on what I did—and "sinful passions [are] aroused by the law" (Romans 7:5). Whenever we commit ourselves to a program, rules, method, principles, and so on to perform, we put ourselves under law, and the law is what gives sin power in our lives (1 Corinthians 15:56). Paul didn't ask, "*What* will set me free?" but "*Who* will set me free?" (Romans 7:24). There is no "what" (program, method, you name it)—nothing you can do that can set you free, but "if the Son sets you free, you will be free indeed" (John 8:36).

Declaration of Deliverance, Freedom, and Victory in Christ

Lord, I thank You that I, _____, who have stumbled, sinned, struggled, fumbled, faltered, and failed so many times, am completely forgiven, totally accepted, and unconditionally loved with an unending and limitless love by You. I'm not a sinner and I'm not an addict, but a child of God—and I am justified and sanctified in the name of the Lord Jesus Christ and by the Spirit of our God (1 Corinthians 6:11). I am dead to sin, freed from it, and alive to You (Romans 6:8,11), holy, righteous, and blameless because of what Christ has done (Ephesians 5:27). All of my sins past, present, and future have been paid for (Colossians 2:13). When Jesus said, "*It is finished*" (John 19:30), He meant it.

I am free forever from condemnation, judgment, shame, guilt, and punishment (Romans 8:1). The last judgment for the Christian was at the cross. Sin is no longer an issue. The only issue in my life is my relationship with Christ. I don't focus on what to do or not do, but on Jesus who is in me. I am united with Christ and He is one with me (1 Corinthians 6:17). I don't try anything, attempt anything, or intend anything; I simply accept the fact that I am accepted and trust Christ as my life (Colossians 3:4). I am not under law, but under grace (Romans 6:14), and I've been set free to live a free life (Galatians 5:1). I don't submit to rules, steps, principles, or regulations as they have no power against the desires of the flesh (Colossians 2:20,23). I submit to God and resist the devil, knowing that he will flee from me (James 4:7). I'm released from the law, its demands, people's opinions, religious systems, and church traditions and now live in the new life of the Spirit (Romans 7:6). No matter what I do or don't do, God is going to love, accept, and bless me throughout all eternity.

I am complete in Christ (Colossians 2:10) and can't get any more complete than that. God has given me everything I need for life and godliness by knowing Jesus, and He has given me His very great and precious promises that I may participate in the divine nature and escape the corruption in the world caused by evil desires (2 Peter 1:3-4). I'm a joint heir with Christ (Romans 8:17). God is for me, so who can be against me? He gave up His only Son for me, and will give me all things (Romans 8:31-32).

The old sin-loving sinner I was has been crucified and is dead and buried (Romans 6:4-6). I have been raised up with Christ and am a new creation (2 Corinthians 5:17). Christ lives in me, and I live by faith in the Son of God who loved me and gave Himself for me (Galatians 2:20). Because of His great love for me God made me alive in Christ even when I was dead in my sins (Ephesians 2:4-5). I have been given a spirit of wisdom and revelation into the knowledge of Christ. His immeasurable power for me and in me is the power that raised Christ from the dead.

God has raised me up with Christ and seated me with Him far above all rule and authority, power and dominion, and has put all things under Christ's feet and made Him head over everything (Ephesians 1:17-21). So all things (problems, trials, opposition, and setbacks) are under my feet since I am in Christ, and God causes all things to work together for my good (Romans 8:28). I am born of God, and the evil one cannot touch me (1 John 5:18). Greater is He who is in me than he who is in the world (1 John 4:4). I have been delivered from my besetting sin and am set free to live in a personal, intimate, face-to-face relationship with Jesus with no space between us.

If I fail, I realize that I am not acting according to my true identity in Christ and it's not me but sin in me that is doing it (Romans 7:17). This doesn't affect God's love and acceptance of me, and I confess my sin and thank God I am forgiven. As my flesh continually fights against the Spirit in me (Galatians 5:17), I cast out thoughts opposed to God in me in every situation and take captive every thought to the obedience of Christ and think truth (2 Corinthians 10:4-5).

I am rooted and grounded in His love, and I understand how wide and long and high and deep is the love of Christ that surpasses knowledge that I may be filled with all the fullness of God (Ephesians 3:16-19). No charge can be brought against me. No one can condemn me (Romans 8:33-34). No matter what comes my way—affliction, trouble, persecution, or danger—overwhelming victory is mine through Christ who loves me (Romans 8:35,37). My fears for today, my worries about tomorrow, and even the powers of hell can't keep God's love away (Romans 8:38-39). So I can love and accept others as God accepts me.

Thank You, God, that You have given me the victory (1 Corinthians 15:57) and I don't have to achieve it, but believe it and receive it (1 John 5:4). I have received the abundance of grace and the free gift of righteousness and reign in life through Christ, my Lord, my Savior, and my life (Romans 5:17). Lord, You are the One who has called me, and You are faithful and You will do it (1 Thessalonians 5:24). Your grace is enough. It is all I need for now and all eternity. Your power is made perfect in my weakness and limitations (2 Corinthians 12:8-9). I am invincible, bulletproof, victorious, and free in Christ.

Now to Him who is able to do immeasurably more than all I can ask or imagine according to His power that is at work in me—to Him be glory in the church and in Christ throughout all ages, forever and ever. *Amen!* (Ephesians 3:20-21).

The Way to Live the Victorious Christian Life

STOP trying to make it happen and get it done and

Be still before the LORD *and wait patiently for him (Psalm 37:7).*

STOP focusing on yourself, your issues, your needs, your problems, your sin and

Let us fix our eyes on Jesus, the author and perfecter of faith (Hebrews 12:2).

STOP trying to do right and not do wrong and not sin and

Count yourselves dead to sin but alive to God in Christ Jesus (Romans 6:11).

STOP being anxious about your circumstance and your situation and

Cast all your anxiety on him because he cares for you (1 Peter 5:7).

STOP trying to be good, act like a good Christian, and do good works, because

Those who enter God's rest also cease from their labors as God did from his (Hebrews 4:10).

STOP trying to improve yourself and be a better person and know that

In Him you have been made complete (Colossians 2:10).

STOP trying to get ahead, do more, and advance yourself and

Do not concern yourself with great matters or things too wonderful (Psalm 131:1).

STOP worrying, being agitated, and being troubled about anything or any one and

Do not be anxious about anything, but in every situation, by prayer and petition, with thanksgiving, present your requests to God (Philippians 4:6).

STOP criticizing and judging others and trying to change them and

Accept him whose faith is weak, without passing judgment (Romans 14:1).

STOP trying to overcome your besetting sin or addiction and know that

You have been set free from sin and have become slaves of God (Romans 6:22).

STOP fantasizing about what you would like to have that you don't, and let

Christ take control of you, and don't think of ways to indulge your evil desires (Romans 13:14).

STOP pursuing sanctification and believe that

Faithful is He who calls you, and He also will bring it to pass (1 Thessalonians 5:24).

STOP striving, straining, and struggling to live the Christian life and know

I have been crucified with Christ and I no longer live, but Christ lives in me. The life I now live in the body, I live by faith in the Son of God, who loved me and gave himself for me (Galatians 2:20).

STOP whatever you are doing to try to live the Christian life and trust

Christ, who is your life (Colossians 3:4).

STOP and

Come to Me, all you who are weary and burdened, and I will give you rest. Take my yoke upon you and learn from me, for I am gentle and humble in heart, and you will find rest for your souls. For my yoke is easy and my burden is light (Matthew 11:28-30).

Grace Walk
Recovery Resources

Freedom from Addiction by Neil T. Anderson and Mike and Julia Quarles. Describes Mike's journey from addiction to freedom and the truth that set him free and Julia's deliverance from codependency.

Freedom from Addiction Workbook by Neil T. Anderson and Mike and Julia Quarles. An intensive inductive Bible study of the truth that sets you free. Includes an in-depth look at the influences and lies that shaped and developed Mike's and Julia's strongholds and addictions.

One Day at a Time by Neil T. Anderson and Mike and Julia Quarles. A 120-day devotional that covers the ten topics that need to be addressed for a person to find their freedom. Each devotional is two to three pages long with questions and room to journal at its end.

Overcoming Addictive Behavior by Neil T. Anderson and Mike Quarles. A 150-page book that clearly and concisely tells how to overcome addictive behaviors.

Freedom from Addictive Behaviors Conference DVDs with nine messages by Mike and Julia on how to get free, live free, and stay free from addictive behaviors. Includes 43-page manual.

Freedom from Addictive Behaviors Conference manual.

Freedom from Addiction DVD Seminar. Neil T. Anderson and Mike and Julia Quarles introduce each of the ten sections of the *Freedom from Addiction Workbook*.

Leader's Guide with Group Discussion Questions for the *Freedom from Addictive Behaviors Conference* DVDs.

"Looking for Love in All the Wrong Places" and "All Our Problems Are Solved at the Cross." Two messages by Mike Quarles on DVD.

Freedom in Christ Recovery Bookmark. With "Who I Am in Christ" on one side and "The Overcomer's Covenant in Christ" on the other.

"The Key to the Victorious Christian Life" by Mike Quarles. The key to being free and walking free. 15-page booklet.

Testimonies of Mike and Julia Quarles. How they found their freedom. Free.

Left Behind by Mike Darnell. A great book on God's unconditional love, identity in Christ, a proper concept of God, and why forgiveness is essential to freedom.

Grace Walk Conference. The foundational conference (eight hours), in which Steve McVey teaches the biblical message of who we are in Christ and how we can live from that reality.

Grace Walk by Steve McVey. Tells Steve's story of how he came to the end of himself and moved from legalism to grace. Includes foundational information on what he learned.

Grace Walk Experience. A workbook by Steve McVey that goes more deeply into the material from *Grace Walk*.

For more information, prices, and how to order,
*go to **freedomfromaddiction.org** or **gracewalk.org***
or contact our office (information on page 199).

More books, DVDs, and audio resources
*are available at **gracewalk.org**.*

What Grace Walk Recovery Ministry Can Offer Your Church or Recovery Ministry

Freedom from Addictive Behaviors Conference

A conference for those struggling with an addictive behavior and for the ones who love them. Also offered as a webinar—Freedom from Addictive Behaviors Basic Webinar—at no charge.

Attendees can find freedom from

- life-controlling problems and habitual sins
- addiction and codependency
- anger and bitterness
- perfectionism and workaholism
- performance-based acceptance and low self-esteem
- eating disorders and irrational fears
- sexual addiction and pornography
- stress and anxiety

The conference consists of eight sessions, and the Basic Webinar covers the first six sessions:

1. *"The Strange Odyssey of a Legalistic Preacher Who Became a Drunk, Discovered Grace, and Was Set Free."* Mike Quarles's testimony of how he found freedom from the bondage of addiction.
2. *"The Problem of Addiction."* A biblical understanding of the problem of bondage (addiction).

3. *"The Price for Freedom."* The requisite for experiencing freedom and why so few are experiencing it.

4. *"God's Answer for Addiction."* God's clear, definitive, and complete answer for bondage (addiction).

5. *"Strongholds of Addiction."* The lies people believe that keep them in the bondage of addiction.

6. *"Forgiveness: Your #1 Ticket to Freedom."* The hardest and most liberating thing you will ever do.

7. *"How to Walk Free and Stay Free."* How to walk in freedom by renewing your mind.

8. *"The Basics of Recovery to Freedom in Christ."* A summary of the truth that sets and keeps you free.

All sessions are illustrated via PowerPoint.

The conference is usually held on Friday night and during the day Saturday. It is also available on DVDs and includes a 43-page manual.

Grace Walk Recovery Ministry Leadership Training Seminar

Also offered as the Freedom from Addictive Behaviors Advanced Webinar, this eight-session seminar covers each section of the *Freedom from Addiction Workbook* with the goal of equipping the attendee to understand that addiction is a spiritual stronghold and to understand the truth that sets you free, so they can help those struggling with addictive behavior to find true and lasting freedom in Christ.

The ten sections covered are listed below. In the Advanced Webinar, sessions 6 and 8 are combined in one session, as are sections 9 and 10.

1. *"How You Got Where You Are."* Understanding how addiction develops and how people got there.

2. *"What Keeps You in Bondage."* Understanding that truth sets you free and lies keep you in bondage.

3. *"Giving Up on Self."* Understanding that coming to the end of self is the prerequisite to finding freedom.

4. *"Understanding the Gospel and Your Heavenly Father."* Understanding that God's love for us is unconditional because He is love, and acquiring a proper concept of our heavenly Father.

5. *"Our Identity in Christ."* Understanding the power and freedom of who we are *in Christ.*

6. *"Freedom from Fear."* Learning to live free from fear, and by faith choosing to cast all our cares upon Him and not worry about tomorrow.

7. *"Freedom from the Past and Victory over Sin."* Understanding that because of the finished work of Christ on the cross we are free from sin; it is no longer our master because we are not under law, but under grace.

8. *"Freedom from Performance-Based Acceptance."* We're completely accepted by God, and He is going to love us through all eternity regardless of what we do or don't do.

9. *"The Battle for the Mind."* Learning the truth that sets you free and keeps you free.

10. *"Growing in Grace."* Understanding that growth and maturity take place not from our sincere efforts, but as we grasp that we are under grace and live by faith in the power of the Holy Spirit.

All sessions are illustrated via PowerPoint.

The webinar version is offered quarterly. It is free, but to gain full benefit, the Freedom from Addiction *book and* Freedom from Addiction Workbook *should be purchased.*

This training can be done in five two-hour sessions following the Freedom from Addictive Behaviors Conference. If you are in the Atlanta area, the training can be done over five weekly sessions.

Guidelines for Group Leaders

1. First and foremost, every leader should have gone through the training. We don't want to be legalistic about this, but it is for your benefit and to enable you to point people to the truth that will set them free. If there is no one who has been trained, but there is someone who is going through the training, that would be okay. If they are going through the training they will have access to receive encouragement and advice, and we encourage them to do so.

2. It is essential that the focus be on the answer—which is the truth that sets free. People should be encouraged to share their problems and where they're at, but you don't want to let the primary focus be on listening to war stories and problems. Unfortunately, some people never get past this. Your biggest challenge will be to bring the discussion back to God's answer, which is freedom in Christ. Don't cut people off from sharing what is going on in their life, but gently and positively bring the discussion back around to the truth, which is Jesus and the freedom He has provided for us. Many people believe they have to analyze the problem to death, but there is no real lasting help in this.

3. This is not a secular support group that helps people cope with their problems. It is not even a Christian 12-Step group that focuses on people working the steps. In the beginning and when you feel it is needed, go over the "Guidelines for Group Discussion and Sharing" that appears in a few pages. A Grace Walk Recovery Group is not like most support groups people have attended, and they need to be reminded that the purpose of the group is to focus on God's answer for addiction. Some are not looking for this type of group, and that is fine.

4. Another challenge will be to not let some people take over the discussion and the meeting. There are some who will talk endlessly about themselves and their problem if given a chance. It will ruin the group if you let them do it. Try to be gentle and not offend them, but remind them the purpose is to give others a chance to share and focus on the answer. You may have to do this several times. If this doesn't work, speak to them outside the meeting. Go over the "Guidelines for Group Discussion and Sharing" with them. If they are not in agreement, you can suggest that this might not be the group they feel they need.

5. Our ministry is not to fix anyone or hold them accountable for their behavior. *Do not* tell people what they should or should not do, even if they are living in gross sin. We cannot make anyone do anything, and to try to do so is counterproductive. Our ministry is to accept them just the way they are, share the truth that sets free, and point them to the One who is the Truth. Don't play the role of the Holy Spirit in another person's life. Our ministry is for reconciliation with God, who has the power to change anyone (see 2 Corinthians 5:17-21).

If you believe it would be helpful for a person to read something or make use of some other resource, it is best to suggest it personally outside the group. Regardless of what they have done or where they have been, keep telling them the truth in love of what Christ has done for them, who they are in Christ, and what He has given them. Remember that people cannot do right until they know the truth of who they are in Christ and what He has done for them. It is not that difficult to help people. Be familiar with and stick to the basics.

6. Some will try confusing the issue with different theological interpretations of Scripture, thus getting you off on rabbit trails. Don't go along with this. In almost every case, this is not the issue. They just want to sidetrack you so they don't have to consider their issues. It is probably best to respond with something like this: "I'm not a biblical scholar but a student. I couldn't say for sure exactly what that means, and that is not our purpose here. I do know that freedom in Christ is available for everyone, and that is what we are here to consider and discuss. This is not a Bible study, but a support group to share the truth that sets free from addiction."

7. Don't think that your job is to have all the answers. No one has a corner on the truth; we are all students and learners. If you have gone through the training, you know what you need to know to lead a group and direct them to the truth that sets free. You know Jesus and what He has done for you—and will do for them. Boldly speak the truth in love and point them to Him, who is the answer, but never argue with anyone or be condescending toward them.

Please contact our office (see page 199)
if you need advice concerning the ministry.

Prayers to Begin and End Recovery Meetings

Prayer to Begin Meeting

We pray constantly, asking God, the glorious Father of our Lord Jesus Christ, to give us spiritual wisdom and understanding, so that we might grow in our knowledge of God. We pray that our hearts will be flooded with light so that we can understand the wonderful future he has promised to those he called. We want to realize what a rich and glorious inheritance he has given to his people. We pray that we will begin to understand the incredible greatness of his power for us who believe him. This is the same mighty power that raised Christ from the dead and seated him in the place of honor at God's right hand in the heavenly realms. (Adapted from Ephesians 1:16-20 NLT 1996.)

Prayer to End Meeting

I pray that from his glorious, unlimited resources he will give us mighty inner strength through his Holy Spirit. And I pray that Christ will be more and more at home in our hearts as we trust in him. May our roots go down deep into the soil of God's marvelous love. And may we have the power to understand, as all God's people should, how wide, how long, how high, and how deep his love really is. May we experience the love of Christ, though it is so great we will never fully understand it. Then we will be filled with the fullness of life and power that comes from God. Now glory be to God! By his mighty power at work within us, he is able to accomplish infinitely more than we would ever dare to ask or hope. May he be given glory in the church and in Christ Jesus forever and ever through endless ages. Amen. (Adapted from Ephesians 3:16-21 NLT 1996.)

Appendix K

Guidelines for Group Discussion and Sharing

1. *Don't play the role of the Holy Spirit in another person's life.* In other words, *do not* tell another person what to do or not do. It is not our ministry to change one another, and the fact is we cannot make anyone do anything or change anyone. Our ministry is for reconciliation with God, who has the power to change anyone (see 2 Corinthians 5:17-21).

2. *Feel free to share where you are and what you are struggling with, but don't focus on the problem—focus on the solution (see Hebrews 12:2-3).* This is not a secular therapy group that helps people cope with their problem or become comfortable with their sin. The goal is to encourage people to know how loved and accepted they are by God and to point them to the Truth (Jesus) that sets them free.

3. *Try to be as open as possible to receive truth.* You may be like many people, who think they know the truth. But the reality is that if we really knew the truth and knew what to do, we wouldn't be struggling with our problem. Realize that God wants to reveal truth that will enable you to walk free, but you must be open and willing to receive it. Don't be argumentative, but do ask the leader to clarify something if you need to. It is not always easy to receive truth, but be open to receive all that God has for you. He loves you and desires for you to be free.

4. *Respect each person as one who is made in the image of God regardless of where they are at and what they are doing.* "Accept

one another, then, just as Christ accepted you, in order to bring praise to God" (Romans 15:7). We are not accepting or tolerating their behavior but are accepting them as Christ accepted us.

5. *DO NOT TRY TO HOLD ANYONE ACCOUNTABLE FOR THEIR BEHAVIOR.* If you really want to help someone, then help them be accountable to the truth. You can do this by "speaking the truth in love" and pointing them to Jesus, who loves them just the way they are and is the truth that sets us free.

6. *Do not share all the gory details of your struggle.* They are not essential in finding God's answer for your addiction and could be offensive and unhelpful to others. If the group is mixed (male and female)—and some will be—then be particularly careful not to share details of sexual issues.

Guidelines for Mentors

1. *Accept the one you're mentoring just the way they are, no matter what they do or believe.* You will not have a ministry in their lives unless you do this. People don't care what you know until they know that you care. Everyone's greatest need is to be accepted, and when you do this, you are not accepting their behavior, but accepting them as a person, the way God accepts them. "Accept one another, then, just as Christ accepted you, in order to bring praise to God" (Romans 15:7).

2. *It is not up to you to change the person, make them do right, or help them quit drinking or drugging or engaging in other addictive behavior.* Only God can do that. Your job is to point them to Christ, who is the way, the truth, and the life. Don't tell them what to do—tell them the truth that sets free.

3. *It is not up to you to hold them accountable for their behavior (good or bad) or to make sure they have covered the material.* It is up to you to hold them accountable to the truth. You want to remind them of the truth that sets free, who they are, what they have in Christ, and who God is toward them (loving, accepting, and affirming).

4. *When they fail, and most will—and for many it will be numerous times—don't accuse, blame, or shame.* That is the enemy's job. Your job is to remind them of who they are in Christ (perfect, complete, righteous, free, and dead to sin), and to remind them that when they act counter to that truth, their problem is they move into deception and are believing a lie.

5. *Whether they fail or not, you need to follow God's advice in Ephesians 4:29:* "Do not let any unwholesome talk come out of your mouths, but only what is helpful for building others up according to their needs, that it may benefit those who listen." This doesn't mean you don't point out attitudes and actions they have that are detrimental, but always speak the truth in love (Ephesians 4:15).

6. *All addicts have a lot of baggage and hurt.* That's a big part of why they are struggling. Most will need Christ-centered, biblical counseling. For referrals in your area check the website at **aelm.org** for excellent counseling that is grace-oriented and will help them deal with their underlying issues. Be careful in directing them to other Christian counselors, because many tend to be legalistic and focus on behavior modification. When they are ready to go through the Steps to Freedom in Christ (the process of confession and repentance developed by Dr. Neil T. Anderson), check out the website at **ficm.org** for referral to someone who is trained and competent in doing this. Some people will need a residential treatment center. Please contact our office (see page 199) for a list of them. You have to be careful here also, as many of these tend to be legalistic as well.

7. *This is not a ministry for those who are looking for quick results.* There will be many who will fall away. It is easy to get discouraged. But remember, you have an answer, and His name is Jesus. Your job is to point the one you're mentoring to Him and to the truth that sets free. "Let us not become weary in doing good, for at the proper time we will reap a harvest if we do not give up" (Galatians 6:9).

Selecting a Mentor

We are glad you are considering selecting a mentor to encourage you and help point you to the truth that sets free. But please seriously consider the points below and pray about this extremely important step. Do not be in a hurry.

Make sure you believe in and are committed to the truth that Grace Walk Recovery Ministry is proposing and are comfortable with it. If you are not, then it will be best to wait until you are. Attend some more meetings and check out some of the resources. This is not the time to challenge the basic tenets of the ministry. Of course, you should ask questions if you are open and teachable, but if you are not at that point it will not be productive. Do not commit yourself until you are ready.

When you are ready, these are things to consider in selecting a mentor:

- Pray that God will lead you to the right person.
- We believe the best mentors are those who have been through the Grace Walk Recovery Ministry Leadership Training. If no such person is available, it would be best to wait. This is not something to rush into.
- Pick a person who is not struggling with addictive behavior and is free in Christ.
- Choose someone who is open about their past problems and struggles and can relate to you.
- Choose someone who is approachable—someone you believe you could share your problems and issues with, and who is willing to spend time with you.

- *Don't* pick someone just because you like them as a person or they are a friend of yours.
- Certainly don't choose someone because they suggest you select them as a mentor.
- Choose someone who knows who they are in Christ and is committed to the truths that Grace Walk Recovery Ministry sets forth.
- Pick someone who attends the meetings regularly.
- Pick someone who is not legalistic or domineering. Don't pick someone who gives the impression they can fix or straighten you out.

Perhaps this seems like a tall order, but it is really just a description of someone who has discovered who they are in Christ—who has discovered their freedom and has a desire to help others do the same. If no one like this is available, we strongly suggest that you wait. Good things come to those who wait (on the Lord).

There Is Now No "How" for Those Who Are in Christ Jesus

How is defined in the dictionary as "in what manner or way; by what means; a manner or method of doing something." There is no method, formula, method, or way, no principles or steps to *do* anything, get free, or be sanctified. If you look for a way to do right, get better, quit drinking, and so on, the harder you look the worse it will get.

The reason is because now *it is finished* (John 19:30). It has all been done. There is nothing we can do. Scripture is clear that God has taken care of it all. *It is for freedom that Christ has set us free. Stand firm, then, and do not let yourselves be burdened again by a yoke of slavery* (Galatians 5:1). We died with Christ (Romans 6:6). We have been buried with Him (Romans 6:4). We were raised up with Him (Romans 6:5), and the new creation that we are (2 Corinthians 5:17) has been freed from sin (Romans 6:7). Christ is in me and I am in Christ (John 14:20). Christ is my life (Colossians 3:4) and I am complete in Him (Colossians 2:10), and you can't get any more complete than that. I have the full package and lack nothing.

My birthright and inheritance as a child of God is freedom in Christ (John 8:32,36). I am forgiven, justified, and sanctified (1 Corinthians 6:11). God has raised me up with Christ and seated me with Him in the heavenly realms in Christ Jesus (Ephesians 2:6). He has given me the victory (1 Corinthians 15:57), always leads me in triumph (2 Corinthians 2:14—no matter what it looks like, feels like, or seems like), and is working all things for my good (Romans 8:28). Now the only *way* I will do right, avoid wrong, get free, be sanctified, and so on is by faith in Christ as my life. Five hundred years ago

Martin Luther said, "Nothing you *do* helps you spiritually." Only faith in Christ, His Word, and His finished work on the cross helps you.

As long as we search for the "how" to get free, shape up, get our act together, and so on, it always results in futility, frustration, and failure, because there is no "how." There are well-meaning people who will give you a "how" and provide you with ways, methods, principles, steps, and so on, but the moment you adopt them you have put yourself under law. When will we learn that the *power of sin is the law* (1 Corinthians 15:56) and that *the law arouses sinful passions* (Romans 7:5)? As long as we believe there is a "how," we believe a lie. Truth sets us free (John 8:32) and lies keep us in bondage. Jesus said *I am the way and the truth and the life* (John 14:6). He didn't come to show us a way to do what we needed to do—pray, read our Bibles, go to church, do right, and abstain from sin. He is the WAY. He didn't come to teach us biblical principles and correct theology so we would know what to do. He is the TRUTH. He didn't come to shape us up and give us a better way of life. He is the LIFE. He came to kill the old sin-loving sinner that was you and give you a new life—HIS LIFE. He lives in you. What else could we possibly need?

He has given us everything we need for life and godliness (2 Peter 1:3). He has given us Himself. What more do we want? If someone tells you that you need something else, consider it bad advice at best and heresy at worst. He has given us His magnificent and precious promises, and we can choose to believe and take Him at His word that *we partake of the divine nature* He has given us (Christ's life) and *escape the corruption in the world caused by evil desires* (2 Peter 1:3-4).

So what should our response be? It could be, "Lord, I don't really feel like it, look like it, or act like it, but I thank You that it is true. Thank You that You have done it all and there is nothing left for me to do. I choose to trust You, depend on You, and rely on You and Your life in me, which is my life. I choose to believe that truth is what You say, regardless of my feelings or actions. I determine to know nothing except Jesus Christ and Him crucified (1 Corinthians 2:2). I thank You. I praise You. I worship You."

To Contact Mike Quarles:

Mike Quarles
Grace Walk Recovery Ministry
4590 Mountain Creek Dr.
Roswell, GA 30075

Phone / fax 770-998-6487

E-mail: freedfrom@centurytel.net
Website: www.freedomfromaddiction.org

To Contact Steve McVey:

Steve McVey
Grace Walk Ministries
PO Box 3669
Riverview, FL 33568

Phone: 800-GRACE 11

E-mail: info@gracewalk.org
Website: www.gracewalk.org

Also by Steve McVey

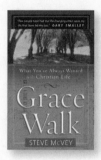

Grace Walk
What You've Always Wanted in the Christian Life

Nothing you have ever done, nothing you could ever do, will match the incomparable joy of letting Jesus live His life through you. It is what makes the fire of passion burn so brightly in new believers. And it is what causes the light of contentment to shine in the eyes of mature believers who are growing in grace.

As you relax in Jesus and delight in His love and friendship, you'll find that He will do more *through you* and *in you* than you could ever do for Him or for yourself. Today is the day to let go of doing and start *being* who you are. Today is the day to start experiencing the grace walk.

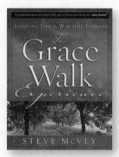

The Grace Walk Experience
Enjoying Life the Way God Intends

"Make sure you're in the Word." "Have a quiet time every day." "Rededicate yourself." "Make a commitment." "Just stop sinning!" Your frustration may be the catalyst God wants to use—right here, right now—to give you a gloriously new understanding of the Christian walk.

Take a deep breath and relax through eight weekly, interactive studies from Steve McVey that show you…

- why it's all right to give up on yourself and your efforts
- how to leave behind a performance- and fear-based faith
- ways to quit "doing" for God, so He can live through you
- how to view the Bible, salvation, and evangelism from a new perspective
- how to be free to enjoy God and the abundant life He's given you

Superb for small-group discussions, church classes, and individual study.

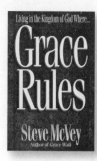

Living in the Kingdom of God Where…
Grace Rules

Are you "living by the rules"…or are you letting God's grace rule you?

There's a big difference. If you're living *for* God—living by the rules—you'll always be exhausted. You'll feel as if you're not doing enough for Him…and that if you don't "measure up," He'll be displeased with you.

But God never meant for you to live the Christian life that way! His love for you isn't based on how you perform for Him. He sent Christ to set you free from rules. He didn't call you to serve Him in your own feeble power…but to let *His* limitless power flow through you!

What's more, this power is available to you right now. God has provided everything you need for a truly meaningful, joy-filled life here on earth…all because of His marvelous grace. Find out how to rest in that grace and let Him live through you in *Grace Rules*.

Other Harvest House Books to Help You Grow

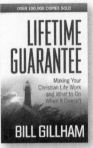

Lifetime Guarantee
*Making Your Christian Life Work and What
to Do When It Doesn't*
BILL GILLHAM

You've tried fixing your marriage, your kids, your job.
Suddenly the light dawns. It's not your problems that
need fixing, it's your life!

In this remarkable and deeply scriptural book you'll
encounter the good news that the Christian (you) is backed by God's lifetime
guarantee...and just what that means for you now, tomorrow, and forever.

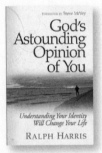

God's Astounding Opinion of You
Understanding Your Identity Will Change Your Life
RALPH HARRIS

Do you know that God's view of you is much greater than
your own? Ralph Harris, founder and president of Life-
Course Ministries, leads you to embrace the Scriptures'
truth about what God thinks of you—that you are special to Him, blameless, pure, and lovable.

With clear and simple explanations and examples, this resource will help you
turn toward the love affair with God you were created for...a relationship in
which you

- exchange fear and obligation for delight and devotion
- recognize the remarkable role and strength of the Holy Spirit
  in your daily life
- view your status as a *new creation* as the "new normal"—and
  live accordingly!

*"Reading this book will change the way you think about yourself, God,
the Christian life, and maybe a few other things along the way!"*

DAVID GREGORY
AUTHOR OF THE BESTSELLING *DINNER WITH A PERFECT STRANGER*

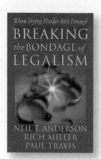

Breaking the Bondage of Legalism
When Trying Harder Isn't Enough
NEIL T. ANDERSON, RICH MILLER, AND PAUL TRAVIS

The Bible talks about it. You see others experiencing it—a Christian life that goes beyond fearful, grit-your-teeth obedience...a rich, *joyful* life. Here, in the personal stories of many believers, you'll find encouragement to come home to your Father—the One who longs for your presence and invites you to enter into His deep love. Scriptural insights from the authors will help you understand

- the bondage that results from legalism
- God's path of hope and liberation
- the joyful intimacy you can now experience with God your Father and Jesus your Friend

Knowing the Heart of the Father
Four Experiences with God That Will Change Your Life
DAVID ECKMAN

You're stuffed full of Christian information. But where is God in all of it?

Perhaps Christianity seems irrelevant to where your heart is really at. Maybe you're thirsting for a *felt experience* of the Bible's truth. What if you could...

1. have an all-encompassing sense that you have a loving heavenly Dad?
2. have a sense of being enjoyed and delighted in by Him?
3. recognize that He sees you differently than you see yourself?
4. realize that *who you are* is more important to Him than *what you do*?

Do you want things to be different? See how these four great heart/soul transformations result in a vibrant, living faith that can stand up to the tests of life.

> *"David Eckman is a man you can trust...*
> *His teaching resonates with God's wisdom and compassion."*
>
> STU WEBER
> AUTHOR OF *TENDER WARRIOR* AND *FOUR PILLARS OF A MAN'S HEART*

To learn more about Harvest House books and
to read sample chapters, log on to our website:

www.harvesthousepublishers.com

HARVEST HOUSE PUBLISHERS
EUGENE, OREGON